VENUS

BY

SUZAN-LORI PARKS

★

★

DRAMATISTS
PLAY SERVICE
INC.

VENUS was produced by The Joseph Papp Public Theater/New York Shakespeare Festival (Goerge C. Wolfe, Producer) in conjunction with Yale Repertory Theatre (Stan Wojewodski, Jr., Artistic Director) at The Joseph Papp Public Theater in New York City, on March 28, 1996. It was directed by, and the set design was by Richard Foreman; the costume design was by Paul Tazewell; the lighting design was by Heather Carson; the original music was by Phillip Johnston; the production dramaturgs were Shelby Jiggetts and Tom Sellar; and the production stage manager was Lisa Porter. The cast was as follows:

MISS SARTJE BAARTMAN, A.K.A. THE GIRL,
    later THE VENUS HOTTENTOT .... Adina Porter
THE MAN, LATER THE BARON
    DOCTEUR.. Peter Francis James
THE BROTHER, LATER THE MOTHER-SHOWMAN,
    LATER THE GRADE-SCHOOL CHUM ...... Sandra Shipley
THE NEGRO RESURRECTIONIST .... Mel Johnson, Jr.
THE CHORUS ...... Cedric Harris, Ben Shenkman, Kevin Isola,
               Lynn Hawley, Thomas Jay Ryan, Adriane Lenox,
                       Rainn Wilson, John Lathan

VENUS was commissioned by The Women's Project and Productions, Inc. (Julia Miles, Artistic Director).

THE ROLES

MISS SAARTJE BAARTMAN, A.K.A. THE GIRL, AND LATER,
    THE VENUS HOTTENTOT

THE MAN, LATER, THE BARON DOCTEUR

THE MAN'S BROTHER, LATER, THE MOTHER-SHOWMAN,
    LATER, THE GRADE-SCHOOL CHUM

THE NEGRO RESURRECTIONIST

THE CHORUS AS:
    THE CHORUS OF THE 8 HUMAN WONDERS,
    THE CHORUS OF THE SPECTATORS,
    THE CHORUS OF THE COURT,
    THE CHORUS OF THE 8 ANATOMISTS,
    THE PLAYERS OF *FOR THE LOVE OF THE VENUS*

Within VENUS are scenes from *FOR THE LOVE OF THE VENUS*, a Drama in Three Acts.

THE CHARACTERS

The Father
The Mother
The Young Man
The Uncle
The Bride-To-Be (later, guised as "The Hottentot Venus")

LIST OF SCENES

5

AUTHOR'S NOTES

From *The Elements of Style.*

In *Venus* I'm continuing the use of my slightly unconventional theatrical elements. Here's a road map.

• *(Rest.)* — Take a little time, a pause, a breather; make a transition.

• A Spell — An elongated and heightened *(Rest.)*. Denoted by repetition of figures' names with no dialogue. Has sort of an architectural look:

THE VENUS
THE BARON DOCTEUR
THE VENUS
THE BARON DOCTEUR

This is a place where the figures experience their pure true simple state. While no action or stage business is necessary, directors should fill this moment as they best see fit.

• [Brackets in the text indicate optional cuts for production.]

• (Parentheses around dialogue indicate softly spoken passages (asides; *sotto voce*).)

VENUS

OVERTURE

The Venus facing stage right.

She revolves. Counter-clockwise. 270 degrees.

She faces upstage.

THE NEGRO RESURRECTIONIST.
The Venus Hottentot!

THE BROTHER, LATER THE MOTHER-SHOWMAN, LATER
THE GRADE-SCHOOL CHUM.
The Venus Hottentot!

THE MAN, LATER THE BARON DOCTEUR.
The Venus Hottentot!

(Rest.)   *(The Venus revolves 90 degrees. She faces R.)*
(Rest.)

THE CHORUS.
The Chorus of the 8 Human Wonders!

THE MAN, LATER THE BARON DOCTEUR.
The Man, later
The Baron Docteur!

THE NEGRO RESURRECTIONIST.
The Negro Resurrectionist!

THE BROTHER, LATER THE MOTHER-SHOWMAN.
The Brother, later
The Mother-Showman! later
The Grade-School Chum!

THE NEGRO RESURRECTIONIST.
The Negro Resurrectionist!

THE CHORUS.
The Chorus of the 8 Anatomists!

(Rest.)   *(The Venus revolves 180 degrees. She faces L.)*
(Rest.)

THE MAN, LATER THE BARON DOCTEUR.
The Chorus of the 8 Anatomists!

THE NEGRO RESURRECTIONIST.
The Man, later
The Baron Docteur!

THE MAN, LATER THE BARON DOCTEUR.
The Negro Resurrectionist!

THE BROTHER, LATER THE MOTHER-SHOWMAN.
The Chorus of Spectators!

THE NEGRO RESURRECTIONIST AND THE MAN,
LATER THE BARON DOCTEUR.
The Brother, later
The Mother-Showman! later
The Grade-School Chum!

THE MAN AND THE BROTHER.
The Negro Resurrectionist!

THE BROTHER, LATER THE MOTHER-SHOWMAN.
The Chorus of the Court!

10

ALL.
The Venus Hottentot!
(Rest.)

THE VENUS.
The Venus Hottentot.
(Rest.)
(Rest.)

THE NEGRO RESURRECTIONIST.
I regret to inform you that The Venus Hottentot iz dead.

ALL.
Dead?

THE BROTHER, LATER THE MOTHER-SHOWMAN.
There wont b inny show tonite.

THE CHORUS OF 8 HUMAN WONDERS.
Dead!

THE NEGRO RESURRECTIONIST.
Exposure iz what killed her, nothin on
and our cold weather. 23 days in a row it rained.
Thuh Doctor says she drank too much. It was thuh cold I
    think.

THE MAN, LATER THE BARON DOCTEUR.
Dead?

THE NEGRO RESURRECTIONIST.
Deh-duh.

THE BROTHER, LATER THE MOTHER-SHOWMAN.
I regret to inform you that The Venus Hottentot iz dead.
There wont b inny show tonite.

THE NEGRO RESURRECTIONIST.
Diggidy-diggidy-diggidy-diggidy.

THE BROTHER, LATER THE MOTHER-SHOWMAN.
Im sure yr disappointed.
We hate to let you down.
But 23 days in a row it rained.

THE NEGRO RESURRECTIONIST.
Diggidy-diggidy-diggidy-dawg.

THE MAN, LATER THE BARON DOCTEUR.
I say:
Perhaps,
She died of drink.

THE NEGRO RESURRECTIONIST.
It was thuh cold I think.

THE VENUS.
Uhhhh!

THE CHORUS OF 8 HUMAN WONDERS.
Turn uhway. Dont look. Cover her face. Cover yer eyes.

THE VENUS.
Uhhhh!

[THE CHORUS.
(Drum. Drum. Drum. Drum.)
(Drum. Drum. Drum. Drum.)

A CHORUS MEMBER.
They came miles and miles and miles and miles and miles.
Comin in from all over to get themselves uh look-see.
They heard the drum.

THE BROTHER, LATER THE MOTHER-SHOWMAN.
Drum Drum

THE CHORUS.
(Drum Drum.)]

THE BROTHER/SHOWMAN.	THE CHORUS.
DRUM	(Drum)
DRUM	(Drum)
DRUM	(Drum)
DRUM	(Drum)

THE VENUS.
(I regret to inform you that Thuh Venus Hottentot iz dead.
There wont b inny show tuhnite.)

THE CHORUS.
(Outrage! Its an outrage!)

THE MAN, LATER THE BARON DOCTEUR.
Dead?

THE NEGRO RESURRECTIONIST.
Deh-duh.

THE BROTHER, LATER THE MOTHER-SHOWMAN.
Tail end of r tale for there must be an end
Is that Venus, Black Goddess, was shameles, she sinned or
      else
completely unknowing of r godfearin ways she stood
totally naked in her iron cage.

THE CHORUS OF 8 HUMAN WONDERS.
Shes thuh main attraction she iz
Loves thuh sideshows center ring.
Whats thuh show without thuh star?

THE VENUS.
Hum Drum Hum Drum.

THE CHORUS.
Outrage! It's an outrage!
Gimmie gimmie back my buck!

THE BROTHER, LATER THE MOTHER-SHOWMAN.
Behind that curtin just yesterday awaited:
Wild Female Jungle Creature. Of singular anatomy. Physiqued
in such a backward rounded way that she outshapes
all others. Behind this curtain just yesterday alive uhwaits
a female — creature
an out — of towner
whos all undressed awaiting you
to take yr peek. So youve heard.

ALL.
We've come tuh see your Venus.

THE MAN AND THE BROTHER.
We know youre disuhpointed.
We hate tuh let you down.

THE NEGRO RESURRECTIONIST.
A scene of Love:

THE VENUS.
Kiss me
Kiss me
Kiss me *Kiss*

[THE MAN, LATER THE BARON DOCTEUR.
I look at you, V
and I see Love

THE VENUS.
Uhhhhhh!
Uhhhhhh!

THE CHORUS OF 8 HUMAN WONDERS.
Turn uhway. Dont look. Cover yr face. Cover yr eyes:

THE BROTHER, LATER THE MOTHER-SHOWMAN.
She gained fortune and fame by not wearing a scrap
Hiding only the privates that lipped in her lap.

THE CHORUS OF 8 ANATOMISTS AND THE MAN, LATER
THE BARON DOCTEUR.
Good God. Golly. Lookie-Lookie-Look-at-her.
Ooh-la-la. What-a-find. Hubba-hubba-hubba.

A CHORUS MEMBER.
They say that if I pay uh little more
I'll get tuh look uh little longer
and for uh little more on top uh that
I'll get tuh stand
stand off tuh thuh side
in thuh special looking place

A CHORUS MEMBER.
*(And from there if I'm really quick I'll stick
my hand inside her
cage and have a feel
if no ones looking).*

ALL.
Hubba-hubba-hubba-hubba.

THE VENUS.
Hum Drum Hum Drum]

ALL.
THE VENUS HOTTENTOT
THE ONLY LIVING CREATURE OF HER KIND IN THE
   WORLD
AND ONLY ONE STEP UHWAY FROM YOU RIGHT NOW
COME SEE THE HOT MISS HOTTENTOT
STEP IN STEP IN.

THE VENUS.
Hur-ry! Hur-ry!

ALL.
Hur-ry! Hur-ry!

THE VENUS.
But I regret to inform you that Thuh Venus Hottentot iz
dead.
There wont b inny show tuhnite.

ALL.
Outrage Its an outrage!
Gimmie gimmie back my buck!

THE NEGRO RESURRECTIONIST
Hear ye Hear ye Order Order!

ALL.
The Venus Hottentot iz dead.

THE NEGRO RESURRECTIONIST.
All rise.

A MEMBER OF CHORUS, AS WITNESS.
Thuh gals got bottoms like hot air balloons.
Bottoms and bottoms and bottoms pilin up like
like 2 mountains. Magnificent. And endless.
An ass to write home about.
Well worth the admission price.

A spectacle a debacle a priceless prize, thuh filthy slut.
Coco candy coloured and dressed all in *au naturel*
she likes when people peek and poke.

THE VENUS.
Hum drum hum drum.

THE BROTHER, LATER THE MOTHER-SHOWMAN.
Step in step in step in step in.

THE VENUS.
There wont b inny show tuhnite.

THE MAN, LATER THE BARON DOCTEUR AND THE
CHORUS.
Hubba-hubba-hubba-hubba.

THE VENUS.
She gained fortune and fame by not wearin uh scrap
Hidin only thuh privates that lipped inner lap.

ANATOMIST FROM THE EAST.
I look at you, Venus, and see:
Science. You
in uh pickle
On my library shelf.

THE VENUS.
Uhhhhhh!
Uhhhhhh!
Uhhhhhh!
Uhhhhhh!

ALL.
Order Order Order Order!
(Rest.)

THE NEGRO RESURRECTIONIST.
Tail end of our tale for there must be an end
is that Venus, Black Goddess, was shameles, she sinned or else
completely unknowing of r godfearin ways she stood
totally naked in her iron cage.
She gaind fortune and fame by not wearin a scrap
Hidin only the privates lippin down from her lap.
When Death met her Death deathd her and left her to rot
Au-naturel end for our hot Hottentot.
And rot yes she would have right down to the bone
Had not the Docteur put her corpse in his home.
Sheed a soul which iz mounted on Satans warm wall
While her flesh has been pickled in Sciences Hall.

(Curtain. Applause.)

Scene 31
May I Present to You "The African Dancing Princess"/ She'd Make a Splendid Freak

Southern Africa, early 1800s. The Girl on hands and knees with scrub brush and bucket scrubs a vast a tile floor. She is meticulous and vigorous. The floor shines.

The Man and his Brother walk about. They are deep in conversation.

THE BROTHER.
So yll finance me?
Yes or No.

THE MAN.
Last time you wanted money lets see what wuz it.

18

Damn, it slips my mind nope Ive got it now:
A Menagerie:
"Gods Entire Kingdom All Under One Roof."
A miserable failure.

THE BROTHER.
I didnt know theyd die in captivity.

THE MAN.
Should of figured on that, Man.

THE BROTHER.
I fed and watered them.

THE MAN.
An animal needs more than that but God
you never were a farmer.

THE BROTHER.
Never was never will be.
(Rest.)
Girl, you missed a spot.
(Rest.)

THE NEGRO RESURRECTIONIST.
Scene 31:
May I Present to You "The African Dancing Princess"/
She'd make a Splendid Freak.
(Rest.)

THE BROTHER.
So yll finance me? Yes or No.

THE MAN.
I need to think on it.

THE BROTHER.
Whats there to think on?

.

19

A simple 2 year investment. Back me
and I'll double yr money no lets think big:
I'll tripple it.

THE MAN.
You need a girl. Wholl go all that way to be a dancer?

THE BROTHER.
Finding the girls the easy part.
(Rest.)
That girl for instance.
Shes good. Vigourous and meticulous.

THE MAN.
(You dont know her?)

THE BROTHER.
Cant say I do.
Yll back me, Man? Say yes.

THE MAN.
Scheme #3 remember?
You went to Timbuktu.

THE BROTHER.
What of it.

THE MAN.
Timbuktu to collect wild flowers?
Wild flowers to bring back here.
"Garden Exotica" admission 2 cents.

THE BROTHER.
They didnt take. Our soils too rich.

THE MAN.
I lost my shirt!

THE BROTHER.
And like a lizard anothers grown back in its place. Back me!
This time Ive got a sure thing.
Ive done tons of background research. This schemell bite!

THE MAN.
A "Dancing African Princess"?

THE BROTHER.
The English like that sort of thing.

THE MAN.
(You really dont remember that girl?)

THE BROTHER.
Not from this angle.
(Rest.)
Theres a street over there lined with Freak Acts
but not many dark ones, thats how we'll cash in.

THE MAN.
A "Dancing African Princess."

THE BROTHER.
Im begging on my knees!

THE MAN.
Get up. Youve got it.

THE BROTHER.
Just like a brother!

THE MAN.
I am yr brother.

THE MAN / THE BROTHER.
Heh heh. Heh heh.

THE MAN.
(You really dont remember her?)

THE BROTHER.
Enlighten me.

THE MAN.
(Scheme #1?)

THE BROTHER.
(Marriage with the Hotten-tot — thats-her?)

THE MAN.
Father recognized the joke straight off
but Mother poor thing she still gives you funny looks.
You were barely 12.

THE BROTHER.
Shes grown.

THE MAN.
As they all do.
Big Bottomed Girls. Thats their breed.
You were at one time very into it.

THE BROTHER.
Big Bottomed Girl. A novelty.
Shes vigourous and meticulous.
(Watch this, Brother!)
(Oh, whats her name?)

THE MAN.
Her — ? Saartjie. "Little Sarah."

THE BROTHER.
Saartjie. Lovely. Girl! GIRL!?

THE GIRL.
Sir?

THE BROTHER.
Dance.

THE GIRL.
Dance?

THE BROTHER.
Dance! Come on!
I'll clap time.
(The Brother claps time. The Girl dances.)

THE MAN.
An "African Dancing Princess"?

THE BROTHER.
The Britsll eat it up.
Oh, she'd make a splendid freak.

THE MAN.
A freak?

THE BROTHER.
Thats what they call em
"freaks," "oddities," "curiosities."

THE MAN.
Of course. Of course.

THE GIRL.
Can I stop, Sir?

THE BROTHER.
No no keep up.
Faster! Ha ha!
(I still dont recognize her.)

23

THE MAN.
(She might know you though.
Their kind remember everything.)

THE BROTHER.
(Ive grown a beard since then.)

THE MAN.
Thats true.

THE BROTHER.
Stop dancing. Stop!

THE GIRL.
Stopped.

THE BROTHER.
Girl?

THE GIRL.
Sir.

THE BROTHER.
How would you like to go to England?

THE GIRL.
England! Well.
"England." Whats that?

THE BROTHER.
A big town. A boat ride away.
Where the streets are paved with gold.

THE GIRL.
Gold, Sir?

THE BROTHER.
Come to England. Dance a little.

THE GIRL.
Dance?

THE BROTHER.
Folks watch. Folks clap. Folks pay you gold.

THE GIRL.
Gold.

THE BROTHER.
We'll split it 50-50.

THE GIRL.
50-50?

THE BROTHER.
Half for me half for you.
May I present to you: "The African Dancing Princess!"

THE GIRL.
A Princess. Me?

THE BROTHER.
Like Cinderella.
Shes heard of Cinderella, right?

THE GIRL.
A princess overnight.

THE MAN.
Thats it.

THE BROTHER.
Yd be a sensation!

THE GIRL.
Im a little shy.

THE BROTHER.
Say yes we'll go tomorrow!

THE GIRL.
Will I be the only one?

THE BROTHER.
Oh no, therell be a whole street full.

THE GIRL.
Im shy.

THE BROTHER.
Think of it: Gold!

THE GIRL.
Gold!

THE BROTHER.
2 yrs of work yd come back rich!

THE GIRL.
Id come back rich!

THE BROTHER.
Yd make a mint!

THE GIRL.
A mint! A "mint".
How much is that?

THE MAN.
You wouldnt have to work no more.

THE GIRL.
I would have a house.

I would hire help.
I would be rich. Very rich.
Big bags of money!

THE MAN.
Exactly.

THE GIRL.
I like it.

THE BROTHER.
Its settled then!

THE MAN.
Yr a rascal, brother.

THE GIRL.
Do I have a choice? Id like to think on it.

THE BROTHER.
Whats there to think on? Think of it as a vacation!
2 years of work take half the take.
Come back here rich. Its settled then.

THE MAN.
Think it over, girl. Go on.
Think it all over.

THE BROTHER.
THE GIRL.
THE MAN.
THE BROTHER.
THE GIRL.
THE MAN.

(Rest.)
(Rest.)

THE GIRL.
Hahahaha!

THE MAN.
What an odd laugh.

THE GIRL.
Just one question:
When do we go?

THE BROTHER.
Next stop England!

THE GIRL.
"England"?

THE BROTHER.
England England England HO!

THE GIRL.
"England"?

THE NEGRO RESURRECTIONIST.
Scene #30:
She Looks Like Shes Fresh Off the Boat:

Scene 30
She Looks Like Shes Fresh Off the Boat

THE CHORUS OF THE 8 HUMAN WONDERS.
Whos that?
Who knows?
Not from these parts.
She looks like shes fresh off the boat.

She looks like shes about to cry.
Go up to her say something nice. Cheer her up make her
    feel welcome.
I remember my first day here.
I didnt know which end was up.
And I had jet lag to boot.
Go to her go on be kind
Go to her say something nice.
(Rest.)
I dunno maybe its better to stay quiet
what can anyone say at a time like this?
"Greetings?" "Salutations?" "Everythings coming up roses?"
Right, good luck.
We could stand here and tell her some lies
or the bald truth: that her lifell go from rough to worse.
Or we could say nothing at all.
What difference will it make?
Shes sunk. Theres no escape from this place.

THE GIRL.
Whos there.

THE CHORUS.
No one in particular.
No one you wanna know.

THE GIRL.
Yr not the other dancing Cinderellas are you?

THE CHORUS.
Hardly, Girl. We've got talents
but none youd pay to see.

THE GIRL.
Yr singers?
Yr magicians!

THE CHORUS.
Yll find out soon enough.

29

THE GIRL.
Its dark in here.
(Rest.)
So this is "England."

THE CHORUS.
Bingo.

THE GIRL.
Youve seen the golden avenues.

THE CHORUS.
Oh boy. Youve bit the big one.
I dunno maybe its better to stay quiet.
What can anyone say at a time like this?
"Greetings!" "Salutations!" "Everythings coming up roses!"

THE GIRL.
So happy to make yr aquaintance.
Ive come here to get rich.
Im an exotic dancer. Very well known at home.
My manager is at this very moment securing us a proper
    room.
We're planning to construct a mint, he and me together.

THE CHORUS.
Right, Girl, good luck.
We could stand here and tell her some lies
or the bald truth: that her lifell go from rough to worse.
Yr a fool, Girl!

THE GIRL.
Yr the fools.
Yr the fools!
Huddled in the dark.
Keep yr distance! You smell!
I'd rather sit here by myself than be called names.

THE CHORUS.
I remember my first day here.
I didnt know which end was up.
And I had jet lag to boot.
Poor girl. We shoulda said nothing. Nothing at all.
What difference could it make?
Shes sunk. Sunk like the rest of us.
Welcome welcome to the club, sweetheart.
Theres no escape from this place.

(The Brother enters with food.)

THE BROTHER.
Here, Girl. Eat this.
It isnt much but things right now are tight.
Take it.

THE GIRL.
Thank you.

THE BROTHER.
Here. Have some water.

THE GIRL.
Thank you.

THE BROTHER.
Hungry?

THE GIRL.
A little.

THE BROTHER.
Thingsll pick up soon.

THE GIRL.
When do we get to England, Sir?

THE BROTHER.
This is England! Cant you tell?

THE GIRL.
I wasnt sure.
(Rest.)
Where are the golden streets?

THE BROTHER.
Just around that bend there.
You cant see them from here.

THE GIRL.
Can I go out and take a look?

THE BROTHER.
No no. Dont budge.
You cant. At least not yet.

THE GIRL.
How long will we live in this room, Sir?

THE BROTHER.
2 or 3 days at the most.
Theres an overweight bureaucrat a real fatso
who dont want you in his country.
Im oiling his palms.
Here have more water.

THE GIRL.
Its dark in here.

THE BROTHER.
Tomorrow I'll show you the golden streets

THE GIRL.
I'm hungry and I'm cold.
Its dark in here.

THE BROTHER.
Remember me? From way back when?
About 12 yrs ago?

THE GIRL.
Youve growd a beard other than that
you havent changed.

THE BROTHER.
I wanted you then and I want you now.
Thats partly why we've come here.
So I can love you properly.
Not like at home.

THE GIRL.
Home?
Love?
You oughta take me shopping. I need a new dress.
I can't be presented to society in this old thing.

THE BROTHER.
Tomorrow I'll buy you the town.
For now lift up yr skirt.
There. Thats good.
(She lifts her skirt showing her ass. He gropes her.)

THE GIRL.
I dont —

THE BROTHER.
Relax.
Presenting "The African Dancing Princess!"

THE GIRL.
Hahahaha!
I dont think I like it here.

THE BROTHER.
Relax.
Relax.
Its going to be fantastic.

(They kiss and touch each other. He is more amorous than she.)
(Rest.)

THE NEGRO RESURRECTIONIST.
Footnote #1
(Rest.)
Historical Extract. Category: Theatrical.
(Rest.)
The year was 1810. At one end of town, in somewhat shabby
circumstances, a young woman, native of the dark continent,
bares her bottoms. At the same time but in a very different
place, on the other end of town in fact, we witness a very
different performance.

(Rest.)

Scene 29
Presenting: "For the Love of The Venus"
A Drama in 3 Acts. Act I, Scene 3:

Scene 29
"For the Love of The Venus,"
Act I, Scene 3

*A play on a stage. The Baron Docteur is the only person in
the audience. Perhaps he sits in a chair. It's almost as if
he's watching TV.*

*The Venus stands off to the side. She watches The Baron
Docteur.*

THE BRIDE-TO-BE.
Coffee, darling.

THE YOUNG MAN.
No thank you.

THE BRIDE-TO-BE.
Tea.

THE YOUNG MAN.
No thank you.

THE BRIDE-TO-BE.
Chocolate.

THE YOUNG MAN.
Chocolate. Mmmmm.

THE BRIDE-TO-BE.
Mmmmm?

THE YOUNG MAN.
No *thank* you.

THE BRIDE-TO-BE.
Look! Oh, what a treasure:
Bah-nah-nah.

THE YOUNG MAN.
You *peel* it.

THE BRIDE-TO-BE.
Peel it. Novelty.

THE YOUNG MAN.
Uncle took Dad to Africa.
Showed Dad stuff. Blew Dads mind.

(Rest.)
(The Young Man reads from his notebook.)
"The Man who has never been from his own home is no
Man. For how can a man call himself *Man* if he has not
stepped off his own doorstep and wandered out into the
world.... Visit the world and *Man* he will be."

[THE BRIDE-TO-BE.
Canasta.
Whist?
Crazy 8s?

THE YOUNG MAN.
"When a Man takes his journey beyond all that to him was
hitherto the Known, when a Man packs his baggage and walks
himself beyond the Familiar, then sees he his true I; not in
the eyes of the Known but in the eyes of the Known-Not."]

THE BRIDE-TO-BE.
You wrote me once
Such lovely poetry.

THE YOUNG MAN.
"His place in the Great Chain of Being is then to him and to
all that set their eyes upon him, thus revealed."

THE BRIDE-TO-BE.
"My Love for you is artificial
Fabricated much like this epistle...."
(Rest.)
Such poetry you used to write me.

THE YOUNG MAN.
"Beholding and Beheld as he is seen through the eyes of the
Great Known-Not — taking his rightful place among the
Splendors of the Universe."
(Rest.)

36

(Rest.)

"Among the Splendors of *Gods* Universe" it should be.
Dontcha think?

THE BRIDE-TO-BE.
Aaahh me:
Unloved.

(Curtain. The Baron Docteur applauds.)

Scene 28
Footnote #2

The Negro Resurrectionist holds fast to The Venus' arm. He reads through The Baron Docteur's notebook.

THE NEGRO RESURRECTIONIST.
Footnote #2:
(Rest.)
Historical Extract. Category: Medical. Autopsy report:
(Rest.)
"Her brain, immediately after removal, deprived of the greater part of its membranes, weighed 38 ounces."
(Rest.)
"Her spinal cord was not examined, as it was considered more desirable to preserve the vertebral column intact. The dissection of her nerves, although carefully made, revealed no important deviations from the ordinary arrangement."
(Rest.)
"Her liver weighed 54 and ¾ ounces and was of a ruinous color and slightly fatty."
(Rest.)
"Her gallbladder was small and a little dilated at the *fundus,* being almost cylindrical when distended with air. Length 4

inches."

(Rest.)

"Her stomach was of the usual form. Small intestines measured 15 feet. Spleen was pale in color and weighed 2 and ¼ ounces. Her pancreas weighed 1 and ¾ ounces. Her kidneys were large."

(Rest.)

(He releases The Venus' arm. She flees but doesn't get far. She runs smack into The Mother-Showman.)

Scene 27
Presenting The Mother-Showman and Her Great Chain of Being

THE MOTHER-SHOWMAN.
Strip down.
Strip down come on yr filthy, Girl.
Come on lets move thats it take off every stitch and hand it
    here and pronto!
I'll clean em for ya.
Damn its dark in here.
That scrap too around yr womans parts hand that here too.

THE GIRL.
It dont come off
It stays. Its custom.

THE MOTHER-SHOWMAN.
Fine.
God. He wasnt lying.
You got enough here to make em come running.
Todays my lucky day.

THE GIRL.
Whats that?

38

THE MOTHER-SHOWMAN.
You smell.
So smelly yll make em go running I said.
Good God.
Heres a bucket and a brush.
Take a bath its yr big day today.
Yr gonna be presented to society so to speak.
Scrub down you smell I said.

THE GIRL.
Maam. Who are you?

THE NEGRO RESURRECTIONIST.
Scene 27:
Prestenting The Mother-Showman and Her Great Chain of
Being:

THE MOTHER-SHOWMAN.
Im yr new boss.
Mother Showman and her 8 Amazing Human Wonders!
Yr Number 9.

THE GIRL.
Wheres my Man?
He had a beard.

THE MOTHER-SHOWMAN.
Him? Girl, he skipped town.
Yr lucky I was passing through
good God Girl he wasnt lying, you woulda starved to death or
    worse, been throwd in jail for heh
indecency. But its all right now, dear. Mother-Showmanll
    guard yr Interests.
Yr Secrets are safe with me.
Scrub.
SCRUB!

(The Girl, apart from the others, scrubs herself. The Mother-Showman introduces her Wonders.)

Sound the drum.

(Wonder #3 sounds the drum.)

Step right up come on come in
Step inside come on come see
The most lowly and unfortunate beings in Gods Universe:
Mother-Showmans 9 Human Wonders will dazzle
surprise intrigue horrify ·and disgust.
The 9 lowest links in Gods Great Chain of Being.

THE CHORUS OF 8 HUMAN WONDERS.
Chain Chain Chain.

THE MOTHER-SHOWMAN.
Look sad like yr misfitness hangs heavy on yr mind.
(Rest.)
Come on in in see with yr own eyes what never ever
should have been allowed to live.
The 9 lowest links in Gods Great Bein Chain.

THE CHORUS OF 8 HUMAN WONDERS.
Chain Chain Chain.

THE MOTHER-SHOWMAN.
See one for the price of a penny and a half
or all these 8 for a song!
Step inside come on come see
the ugliest creatures in creativity. Alive!
Alive! And waiting for you just inside.
Come on in in take a look
see a living misfit with yr own eyes.
Take a look at one for just a penny and a half

you can gawk as long as you like.
Waiting for yr gaze here inside
theyre all freaks and all alive.

[THE CHORUS OF 8 HUMAN WONDERS.
When I was birthed intuh this world
Our Father cursed our Mother spat.
SPAT!

THE MOTHER-SHOWMAN.
Sing!

THE CHORUS OF 8 HUMAN WONDERS.
This face of mine thats scary
These blemishes this crooked back
This extra arm uhtop my head
This extra ear this extra leg
This fin that swims out of my rear
These blisters circling my eyes
Passed down tuh me from who knows where
My existence is a curse
You can gawk for a small purse!
(Rest.)
We wonder thuh world.

THE MOTHER-SHOWMAN.
Step up step in to see what God hisself dont wanna look at.
Every day all day theyre on display!
All Alive!
(Rest.)
Uh hehm.
8th being from the bottom, what I call my Wonder One:
The Bearded Gal.
Uh woman furrier than most.
By her Mom and Pops she was rejected
Shes thuh first freak I collected.

WONDER #1.
Pull on my beard!
It's real! It's real!

THE CHORUS OF 8 HUMAN WONDERS.
We wonder thuh world.

THE MOTHER-SHOWMAN.
After One comes Wonder 2 one step closer to the monkeys
Uh Fireman who dines on flame
He claims thuh Devil his creator
But really hails from thuh Equator.

WONDER #2.
I am her most Flame-boyant child!
Im goin tuh Hell! Hell in uh handbasket!

THE MOTHER-SHOWMAN.
Next rung closer to thuh lowest: Wonder 3: Thuh Spotted
    Boy.
Hes covered black and white all patchy
Thuh Lord could not make up his mind
Dont get too close tuh him its catchy.

WONDER #3.
The Good Lord is indecisive!
I'm thuh proof!

THE CHORUS OF 8 HUMAN WONDERS.
We wander
thuh world.

THE MOTHER-SHOWMAN.
Thuh Fat Mans next: 12 hundred pounds, a woman to us all.

WONDER #4.
Feed me.

THE MOTHER-SHOWMAN.
And if his girth does not impress
Ive 2 ladies here joined at thuh hip
Bornd that way theyll die that way
mano a mano lip tuh lip.

WONDERS #5 AND #6.
Mano a mano lip tuh lip.

THE CHORUS OF 8 HUMAN WONDERS.
We wander thuh world.

THE MOTHER-SHOWMAN.
Chain.

THE CHORUS OF 8 HUMAN WONDERS.
Chain.
We wander thuh world: here is thuh Reason
Our funny looks Read as High Treason.

THE MOTHER-SHOWMAN.
Jawohl Jawohl
Step up my Wandering Wunderfuls
and show how Nature takes her toll.
Almost thuh lowest to thuh bottom is a freak called "Mr.
    Privates."
Hes from thuh South
what we carry *down here* he wears up here
in thuh place of his eyes and his nose and his mouth.

WONDER #7.
Horror! Horror!
Horror! Horror!

THE CHORUS.
Chain!
Chain!

THE MOTHER-SHOWMAN.
On the bottom yesterday was the Whatsit, people, #8
So backward that her cyclops eye
will see into yer future.

WONDER #8.
Black its black!
Myeye sees black!

THE CHORUS OF 8 HUMAN WONDERS.
Howuhbouthat?!
Howuhbouthat?!

WONDER #8.
Black its black!
Myeye sees black!

THE CHORUS OF 8 HUMAN WONDERS.
Howuhbouthat?!
Howuhbouthat?!

THE MOTHER-SHOWMAN.]
Foam rage tear at yr clothes, kids!
Show yr stuff! Dont be shy!
Pull out all thuh stops! Big Finish!
Thats it! Thats it! Make yr Mama proud!

*(The Wonders pull out all the stops then they pose in a freakish
tableau.)*

*(The Girl has finished her bath. The Negro Resurrectionist watches
her.)*

THE VENUS.
What you lookin at?

THE NEGRO RESURRECTIONIST.
You.

(Rest.)
Yr lovely.

THE VENUS.
THE NEGRO RESURRECTIONIST.
THE VENUS.
THE NEGRO RESURRECTIONIST.

THE MOTHER-SHOWMAN.
With yr appreciative permission
For a seperate admission
We've got a new girl: #9
the "Venus Hottentot."
She bottoms out at the bottom of the ladder
Yr not a man — until youve hadder.
But truly, folks, before she showd up our little show was in
      the red
But her big bottoms friendsll surely put us safely in the black!

*(The Girl stands in the semi-darkness. Lights blaze on her. She is
now The Venus Hottentot. The Wonders become The Chorus of
Spectators and gather round.)*

THE MOTHER-SHOWMAN.
THE VENUS HOTTENTOT
THE ONLY LIVING CREATURE OF HER KIND IN THE
      WORLD
STEPSISTER-MONKEY TO THE GREAT
LOVE
GODDESS
AND ONLY ONE STEP AWAY FROM YOU RIGHT NOW
COME SEE THE HOT MISS HOTTENTOT
STEP IN STEP IN
HUR-RY! HUR-RY!
HUR-RY! HUR-RY!

THE VENUS.

THE CHORUS OF THE SPECTATORS.
THE VENUS.
THE CHORUS OF THE SPECTATORS.
THE VENUS.
THE CHORUS OF THE SPECTATORS.
THE VENUS.
THE CHORUS OF THE SPECTATORS.

(Rest.)

THE VENUS.
Oh, God:
unloved.
(Rest.)

THE NEGRO RESURRECTIONIST.
Footnote #3:
Historical Extract: Category: Literary: From Robert Chambers'
Book Of Days:
(Rest.)
"Early in the present century a poor wretched woman was
exhibited in England under the appelation of *The Hottentot
Venus*. The year was 1810. With an intensely ugly figure,
distorted beyond all European notions of beauty, she was said
by those to whom she belonged to possess precisely the kind
of shape which is most admired among her countrymen, the
Hottentots."
(Rest.)
The year was 1810, three years after the Bill for the Abolition of
the Slave-Trade had been pased in Parliament, and among
protests and denials, horror and fascination, the Venus show
went on.
(Rest.)

THE VENUS.
THE CHORUS OF THE SPECTATORS.
THE VENUS.
THE CHORUS OF THE SPECTATORS.
THE VENUS.

SPECTATOR #1.
eeeeeeeeeeeeeeeeeeeeeeeeeeeeeeeeeeeeeeeeeeeeeeeeee!

THE MOTHER-SHOWMAN.
Get used to it, Girl.
(Rest.)

THE NEGRO RESURRECTIONIST.
Scene 26:
From "For the Love of The Venus." Act II, Scene 9:

Scene 26
"For The Love of The Venus,"
Act II, Scene 9

As before, The Baron Docteur is its only audience, and The
Venus watches him.

THE BRIDE-TO-BE.
Eeeeeeeeeeeeeeeeeee
he doesnt care
uh whit uhbout meeee.

THE MOTHER.
Dont be a gumball, child.

THE BRIDE-TO-BE.
He turns down tea.
He turns down coffee.
He will not take a turn in the park with me.
He will not hold my hand.

THE MOTHER.
Have you tried whist? He loves his whist.

47

THE BRIDE-TO-BE.
He used to leave me
poetry
In thuh knot of thuh tree in thuh front of my house.

THE MOTHER.
Have you tried canasta?

THE BRIDE-TO-BE.
"My love for you, My Love, is artificial,
Fabricated much like this epistle…"
(Rest.)
"My Love, My Love, My Love, My Love, — "
No more rhymes
Now he writes *tracts.*
Prose essays on *(Africaaaaah!)*

THE MOTHER.
There there girl dont cry.
Have faith in Love. Wipe your nose.
There there thats nice.

THE BRIDE-TO-BE.
Aaaah me: unloved.

(Tableau. The Baron Docteur applauds. Curtain.)

THE NEGRO RESURRECTIONIST.
Counting Down/Counting the Take:

Scene 25
Counting Down/Counting the Take

SPECTATOR #1.
Eeeeeeeeeeeeeeeee!

THE MOTHER-SHOWMAN.
Get used to it, Girl.
We're gonna be rich.
(Rest.)
Can you count?

THE VENUS.
I can count.

THE MOTHER-SHOWMAN.
That puts you a bit above the rest.
But thats our secret.
(Rest.)

THE NEGRO RESURRECTIONIST.
Scene 25:

THE MOTHER-SHOWMAN.
10-20-30-40
50-60-70-80-90:

THE VENUS.
1.

THE MOTHER-SHOWMAN.
10-20-30-40
50-60-70-80-90:

THE VENUS.
2.

THE MOTHER-SHOWMAN.
10-20-30-40
50-60-70-80-90:

THE VENUS.
3.

THE MOTHER-SHOWMAN.
10-20-30-40
50-60-70-80-90:

THE VENUS.
4.

THE MOTHER-SHOWMAN.
10-20-30-40
50-60-70-80-90:

THE VENUS.
5.

THE MOTHER-SHOWMAN.
10-20-30-40
50-60-70-80-90:

THE VENUS.
6.
(Rest.)

THE MOTHER-SHOWMAN.
9 ugly mouths to feed.
Plus my own.
We didnt do too bad today.
Hottentot, yr a godsend!

THE NEGRO RESURRECTIONIST.
31
30
29
28
27
26
25
24:

Scene 24
"But No One Ever Noticed/
Her Face Was Streamed with Tears"

THE CHORUS OF THE 8 HUMAN WONDERS.
Ive been in this line of work for years
and yet everytime the crowds gather and the lights flash up
I freak out.
My first 5 months in this racket were like hell.
I didnt sleep I didnt eat my teeth were chattering non stop.
That girl they call The Venus H. is holding up
holding up pretty well I think. And her crowds have been
    stupendous.
(Some audience is better than none at all and since she's
    come
we're in another economic bracket.) Stupendous!
Stupendous! Still: shes got that far away look in her eye
that look of a someone who dont know the score.
She signed on for 2 years "only 19 months to go" shes
    thinking.
But should I tell her? Uh uhnn, I havent got the heart to say:
"Oh, Venus H., there is absolutely no escape."
(Rest.)
(Rest.)

(An enormous banner unfurls: It reads "THE VENUS
HOTTENTOT " and bears her likeness. The Venus enters C. The
Wonders in the background.)

THE MOTHER-SHOWMAN.
Turn to the side, Girl.
Let em see! Let em see!
(Rest.)
What a fat ass, huh?!
Oh yes, this girls thuh Missin Link herself.

Come on inside and allow her to reveal to you the Great and
     Horrid Wonder
of her great heathen buttocks.
Thuh Missing Link, Ladies and Gentlemen: Thuh Venus
     Hottentot:
Uh warnin tuh us all.
Right this way.
(Rest.)
Sure is slow today.
No one around for miles.
Lets see:
(Rest.)
Plucked her from thuh Fertile Crescent
from thuh Fertile Crescent with my own bare hands!
Ripped her off thuh mammoth lap of uh mammoth ape!
She was uh (((*keeping house for him*))). Folks, The Venus
     Hottentot!
(Rest.)
Yr standing there with yr lips pokin out
like uh wooden lady on uh wooden ship
look uhlive
smile or somethin
jesus
stroke yr feathers
smoke yr pipe.
(Rest.)
Been with us in civilization for a mere 5 months.
Teached her all she knows.
Look! Shes got talents!
(Rest.)
Walk, girl.

(*The Venus walks about.*)

WHAT A BLACKSIDE! OOOH LA LA!
STEP IN!
STEP IN STEP IN STEP IN STEP IN!
(Rest.)

(Rest.)
Dry as a bone today.
(Rest.)
Dance or something.

THE VENUS.
Dance?

THE MOTHER-SHOWMAN.
Dance. Go on Girl and the other uglies you all too.
I'll clap time.
DANCE!

(The Mother-Showman claps time. The Venus and the Wonders dance.)

(Suddenly the Wonders disappear.)

THE NEGRO RESURRECTIONIST.
Footnote #4
Historical Extract: Category: Newspaper Advertisements.

AN ADVERTISING BILL: From Daniel Lysons *Collectanea: of a Collection of Advertisements and Paragraphs from the Newspapers relating to Various Subjects* (London, 1809.)

"Parties of 12 and upwards, may be accommodated with a Private Exhibition of the HOTTENTOT ... between 7 and 8 o'clock in the evening, by giving notice to the Door-Keeper the Day previous.

The HOTTENTOT may also be viewed by single parties with no advance notice from 10 in the morning until 10 in the evening. Mondays through Saturdays. No advance notice is necessary.

A Woman will attend (if required)."

(The Mother-Showman is still clapping time. The Venus is still dancing. Spectator #2 wanders in to watch. He hands over a coin.)

THE MOTHER-SHOWMAN.
Good morning, Sir!
Good morning!
A thousand thanks a million pleasantries
we do appreciate yr audience.

(The Mother-Showman out of breath stops clapping. The Venus stops dancing. Spectator #2 pays some more.)

What a bucket!
What a bum!
What a spanker!
Never seen the likes of that, I'll bet.
Go on Sir, go on.
Feel her if you like.

(He takes a feel. He wanders off. The Mother-Showman wets her finger and tests the wind direction.)

Look extra pitiful, Girl. Yeah thats it.
(Rest.)
Ladies and Gents are you feeling lowly?
Down in the dumps?
Perhaps yr feelin that yr life is all for naught? Ive felt that
    way myself at times.
Come on inside get yr spirits lifted.
One look at thisll make you feel like a King!

(Several Spectators wander in.)

Ladies and Gents: THE VENUS HOTTENTOT
Shes been in civilization a whole year and still hasnt learnd
    nothin!

The very lowest rung on Our Lords Great Evolutionary
      Ladder!
Observe: I kick her like I kick my dog!
Aaah! Aaaah! Aaaah!

*(The Mother-Showman kicks The Venus repeatedly. The act has the
feel of professional wrestling. The Spectators shout approval.)*

THE VENUS.	THE MOTHER-SHOWMAN.
Oh!	Aaaah!
Ah!	Aaaah!
Oh!	Aaaah!
Ah!	

(Out of breath again, The Mother-Showman stops to rest.)

THE MOTHER-SHOWMAN.
Whew. Thats hard work lemmie tell ya.
I need a rest. Hhh.
Paw her folks. Hands on. Go on have yr pleasure.
Her heathen shame is real.

(The Spectators paw The Venus.)

Thuh kicks is native for them Hottentots.
When I was down there in their hot home
As Gods my witness Kickin Kickin
Kickin all day Kickin at eachother
Thats just their way!
They do one kick for our "move uhbout"
2 kicks means uh well "pass thuh meat"
They mix it with thuh toes n heel: uh whole language of
      kicks
very sophisticated
for them of course.
(Rest.)
Verify me, Venus.
(Go on, Girl, nod and back me up)

See? I speak the truth!
Mother-Showman does not lie.
Stand up now, Girl.
Let em see you in yr alltogether.
Stand up thats it let Mother help ya.
Lets give these folks their moneys worth.
Stand still. In profile. There thats nice.
Ladies and Gents:
The Hottentots best angle.

THE CHORUS OF THE SPECTATORS.
THE VENUS.
THE MOTHER-SHOWMAN.
THE CHORUS OF THE SPECTATORS.
THE VENUS.
THE MOTHER-SHOWMAN.
THE CHORUS OF THE SPECTATORS.
THE VENUS.
THE MOTHER-SHOWMAN.

(Rest.)

(The Chorus errupts in wild laughter.)

THE CHORUS OF THE SPECTATORS.
HAHAHAHAHAHAHAHAHAHAHAHAHHAHAHAHAHA
HAHAHHAHAHAHAHHAHAHAHAHHAHAHAHAHA
HAHAHAHAHAHAHAHAHAHAHAHAHAHAHHAHAHHAHA

THE VENUS.
THE VENUS.
THE VENUS.

THE VENUS.
Hahahahahahahaha!

THE NEGRO RESURRECTIONIST.
Footnote #5:

Historical Extract: Category: Literary, from *The Life of One Called The Venus Hottentot as Told By Herself*
(Rest.)
"the things they noticed were quite various
but no one ever noticed that her face was streamed with tears."
(Rest.)
Scene 23: "For the Love of The Venus," Act II, Scene 10

Scene 23
"For the Love of The Venus,"
Act II, Scene 10

Again, The Baron Docteur is the only audience. The Venus watches him.

THE FATHER.
Youre in uh pickle Young Man
An absolute pickle

THE UNCLE.
Nabsolute pickle no question Boy.

THE FATHER.
Marry yr girl, Boy and then
Unclell take ya to Timbuktu
if Timbuktus yr yen.

THE YOUNG MAN.
To Timbuktu?
(Rest.)
A Man to be a Man must know Unknowns! So
if the Man cant sail to the Unknown I guess
the Unknown will sail to the Man. So!
Im all decided:

before I wed, Uncle, I'd like you to procure for me an oddity.
I wanna love
Something Wild.

THE FATHER.
THE UNCLE.
THE YOUNG MAN.

THE UNCLE.
Be a little more specific.

THE YOUNG MAN.
In the paper yesterday:
"In 2 weeks time
For one week only"
Something called "THE HOTTENTOT VENUS"
Uncle. Get her for me somehow.

THE FATHER AND THE UNCLE.
Heh. Heh.
Heh. Heh.

THE YOUNG MAN.
Im all decided.

THE FATHER.
(Make sure shes not *too* strange, brother.
Brother, make sure shes clean.)

THE UNCLE.
In 2 weeks time!
I will present to you, Young Man:
New Love!

(Tableau. The Baron Docteur applauds. Curtain.)

Scene 22
Counting the Take/The Deal That Was

THE VENUS.
10-20-30-40
50-60-70-80-90:

THE MOTHER-SHOWMAN.
22.

THE VENUS.
10-20-30-40
50-60-70-80-90:

THE MOTHER-SHOWMAN.
23.

THE VENUS.
10-20-30-40
50-60-70-80-90:

THE MOTHER-SHOWMAN.
24.

THE VENUS.
10-20-30-40
50-60-70-80-90:

THE MOTHER-SHOWMAN.
25.

THE VENUS.
You hit me hard the other day.

THE MOTHER-SHOWMAN.
Mothers sorry.

THE VENUS.
We should spruce up our act.
I could speak for them.
Say a little poem or something.

THE MOTHER-SHOWMAN.
Count!

THE VENUS.
You could pretend to teach me and I would learn
before their very eyes.

THE MOTHER-SHOWMAN.
Yr a negro native with a most remarkable spanker.
Thats what they pay for.
Their eyes are hot for yr tot-tot.
Theres the poetry.

THE VENUS.
We should expand.

THE MOTHER-SHOWMAN.
Count!!

THE VENUS.
(Rest.)
10-20-30-40
50-60-70-80-90:

THE MOTHER-SHOWMAN.
26.

THE VENUS.
10-20-30-40
50-60-70-80-90:

THE MOTHER-SHOWMAN.
27.

THE VENUS.
10-20-30-40
50-60-70-80-90:

THE MOTHER-SHOWMAN.
28.

THE VENUS.
10-20-30-40
50-60-70-80-90:

THE MOTHER-SHOWMAN.
29.

THE VENUS.
10-20-30-40
50-60-70-80-90:

THE MOTHER-SHOWMAN.
30.

THE VENUS.
10-20-30-40
50-60-70-80-90:

THE MOTHER-SHOWMAN.
31. And change.
Hhhhh.
We didnt do too bad today.
(Rest.)
(Rest.)
A Whirlwind Tour! 100 cities in as many nights!
It sounds like fun.
Lets see now:

(The Mother-Showman consults her map.)

Town X to Town Y Town Y to Town Z.
Town Z to Town A Town A to Town B.
Town B to Town C then back to Town X then off
to Town hmmmmm.

THE VENUS.
THE MOTHER-SHOWMAN.
THE VENUS.

THE MOTHER-SHOWMAN.
Dont steal from me, girl.
Yll go to hell for it.

THE VENUS.
Hell?

THE MOTHER-SHOWMAN.
Christian talk. Fire and brimstone and Satan himself.
Very hot.

THE VENUS.
Oh.

THE MOTHER-SHOWMAN.
Put thuh money back.

THE VENUS.
You pay us each 5 coins a week.
We're all paid equal
but we dont draw equal.

THE MOTHER-SHOWMAN.
Its past yr bedtime, daughter.

THE VENUS.
I'm thuh one they come to see.
I'm thuh main attraction.
Yr other freaks r 2nd fiddles.

THE MOTHER-SHOWMAN.
Oh boy: uh Diva.

THE VENUS.
I should get 50 uh week.
Plus better food, uh lock on my door and uh new dress now
    n then.

THE MOTHER-SHOWMAN.
You should get some sleep, girl.
I wake you up early and you never like it.

THE VENUS.
50 uh week good food locked door new clothes say its a deal.

THE MOTHER-SHOWMAN.
Go to hell.

THE VENUS.
40 then, the clothes and my own room. Forget the food.

THE MOTHER-SHOWMAN.
Nothin doin, Lovely.

THE VENUS.
30.

THE MOTHER-SHOWMAN.
Nope.

THE VENUS.
I'm leaving then.

THE MOTHER-SHOWMAN.
Where to?

THE VENUS.
Home.

THE MOTHER-SHOWMAN.
But yr not yet rich and famous.

THE VENUS.
Im not?

THE MOTHER-SHOWMAN.
Yr a little known in certain circles but you havent made yr
    fortune.
Go back home and folks will laugh.
Hahahaha.
Stay.

THE VENUS.
No.
I'll set up shop and show myself.
Be my own Boss make my own mint.

THE MOTHER-SHOWMAN.
Youd walk out on yr mother?

THE VENUS.
My time with you is spent.
2 yrs work
half the take for take-home pay, I'm due at least a thousand
    coins!
That was the deal.

THE MOTHER-SHOWMAN.
That deal you didnt make with me, Love.
You made yr bargin with a man Ive never met!
For all I know youve made him up.
Yeah, yr lyin and tryin to swindle yr poor Mother
out of her retirement.

THE VENUS.
2 yrs work
half the take

him and me were agreed.
Hand it over.

THE MOTHER-SHOWMAN.
Nothin doin.

THE VENUS.
Im out of here.
I'll make my own mark.
Im all decided.

THE MOTHER-SHOWMAN.
"Im all decided" oooh la la.
Could it be Ive been showing you all wrong?
Christ I thought yr name was "Venus" but, Lord of mercy,
Yr the Queen of Fucking Sheeba.

THE VENUS.
Hand it over.

THE MOTHER-SHOWMAN.
Nope.
Go to bed.

THE VENUS.
I want whats mine!

THE MOTHER-SHOWMAN.
They dont let your kind run loose in the streets
Much less set up their own shops.

THE VENUS.
Gimmie!

THE MOTHER-SHOWMAN.
You could be arrested.
You need Mothers protection.

THE VENUS.
GIMMMMMIE!

THE MOTHER-SHOWMAN.
Dont push me, Sweetie.
Next doors a smoky pub
full of drunken men.
I just may invite them in
one at a time
and let them fuck yr brains out.

THE VENUS.
They do it anyway.
(Rest.)
(Rest.)

THE MOTHER-SHOWMAN.
Well.
Its the same
for all of us, Love.

THE VENUS.
They come in drunken when yr sleeping.
(Rest.)
I wanna go.
Please.

THE MOTHER-SHOWMAN.
Home?

THE VENUS.
No.
Not home.

THE MOTHER-SHOWMAN.
Where to, then?

(Rest.)
(Rest.)

THE VENUS.
Innywhere.

Scene 21
The Whirlwind Tour

*During this scene The Baron Docteur watches The Venus
and the others from his chair. He grows more and more
interested and watches more and more intently.*

*The Venus, The Mother-Showman and The Chorus of 8
Wonders stand in a knot.*

They are traveling.

THE NEGRO RESURRECTIONIST.
Town A! Town B! Town C! Town E!
Town 25! Town 36! Town 42! Town 69!

[THE CHORUS OF 8 HUMAN WONDERS.
Legend has it that The Girl was sent away from home.
Those who sent her said she couldnt return for a thousand
    yrs.
Even though she was strong of heart even she doubted she
    would live that long.
After 500 years they allowed her to ask a question.
She wanted to know what her crime had been.
Simple: You wanted to go away once.
9 hundred 99 years were finally up
just one more year to go.
She had in all that time circled the globe twice on foot
saw 12 hunderd thousand cities
and had a lover or 2 in every port.

She spent her last year of banishment living in a cave
carved out outside the city wall.
She spent that whole year longing not looking but longing
    not looking.
They let her back in right on time
all of her friends had died and well
she didnt recognize the place.]

(The Chorus of 8 Wonders disappear. The Venus and The Mother-Showman remain.)

THE NEGRO RESURRECTIONIST.

Town R! Town U! Town E!	THE VENUS.
Town Q!	THE MOTHER-SHOWMAN.
Town 58! Town 64!	THE VENUS.
Town 85! Town 99!	THE MOTHER-SHOWMAN.
(Rest.)	THE VENUS.
(Rest.)	THE MOTHER-SHOWMAN.
Town A! Town B! Town C!	THE VENUS.
Town E!	THE MOTHER-SHOWMAN.
Town 25! Town 36!	THE VENUS.
Town 42! Town 69!	THE MOTHER-SHOWMAN.
(Rest.)	THE VENUS.
Town R! Town U! Town E!	
Town Q!	
Town 58! Town 64!	
Town 85! Town 99!	

THE VENUS.
How many towns till we get home?!

(A knot of Spectators appear.)

THE MOTHER-SHOWMAN.
Presenting
Presenting
Presenting

THE VENUS HOTTENTOT!
Love gone all wrong, if you will.
Uh warning to us all.
Gentlemen, Ladies, get yrselves a good long look.
Kiddies push yr ways up front.

THE CHORUS OF SPECTATORS.
THE VENUS.

THE CHORUS OF SPECTATORS.
(Rest.)
Ooooooooooooooooooooooooooooh!
(Rest.)
(Rest.)
Aaaaaaaaaaaaaaaaaaaaaaaaaaaaaaaaah!
(Rest.)
(Rest.)

THE NEGRO RESURRECTIONIST.
Town 10! Town 3!
Town R! Town Z!
Town X!

THE MOTHER-SHOWMAN.
Uh gift of chockluts is customary.
Place yr treats at her feets and watch her feed.

THE NEGRO RESURRECTIONIST.

Town R! Town U! Town E!	THE VENUS.
Town Q!	THE MOTHER-SHOWMAN.
Town 58! Town 64!	THE VENUS.
Town 85! Town 99!	THE MOTHER-SHOWMAN.
(Rest.)	THE VENUS.
(Rest.)	THE MOTHER-SHOWMAN.
Town A! Town B! Town C!	THE VENUS.
Town E! Town 25! Town 36!	THE MOTHER-SHOWMAN.
Town 42! Town 69!	THE VENUS.

(Rest.)
Town R! Town U! Town E! Town Q!
Town 58! Town 64! Town 85! Town 99!

THE VENUS.
How many towns till we get home?

[THE CHORUS OF SPECTATORS.
Legend has it that The Girl was sent away from home.
Those who sent her said she couldnt return for a thousand
    yrs.
Even though she was strong of heart even she doubted she
    would live that long.
After 500 years they allowed her to ask a question.
She wanted to know what her crime had been.
Simple: You wanted to go away once.
9 hundred 98 of the years were finially up
just 2 short years to go.
She had in all that time circled the globe twice on foot
had 12 hunderd thousand children
and a husband or 2 in every port.
She spent her last 2 years of banishment living in a cave
    carved out
outside the city wall.
She spent those 2 years longing not looking but longing not
    looking.
They let her back in right on time
all of her friends had died and well
she didnt recognize the place.]

(The Mother-Showman cages The Venus.)

THE NEGRO RESURRECTIONIST.
Town R! Town U! Town E! Town Q!
Town 58! Town 64! Town 85! Town 99!

(Rest.)
Town M! Town O! Town P! Town S!
Town 3! Town 5! Town 4! Town 9!

(The Baron Docteur is out of his chair and watching The Venus. He is transfixed.)

THE VENUS.
THE CHORUS OF SPECTATORS.

(The Spectators burst into riot. They beat the The Venus' cage with sticks. They also beat The Mother-Showman.)

THE BARON DOCTEUR.
Order! Order! Order! Order!

Scene 20A
The Venus Hottentot Before the Law
Footnote #5 Historical Extract: Musical.
From R. Toole-Scott *"The Circus and Allied Arts"*

THE NEGRO RESURRECTIONIST.
(Rest.)
A Song of The Hottentot ladie and her day in court and what the judges did therein.

(As The Negro Resurrectionist sings The Spectators lead The Venus to her new cage: a jail cell; and then transform themselves into The Chorus of the Court.)

Have you heard about
the rump she has (though strange it be)
Large as a cauldron pot?
This is why men go to see
The Venus Hottentot.

71

She showd her butts for many a day,
and eke for many a night;
Till fights broke out in our dear streets
Now, this was not all right.
Some said this was with her goodwill
Some said that this was not
All asked why they did use so ill
This lady HOTTENTOT.

At last the sober folks stood forth
And into Court they took her
To thus determine if she liked
For everyone to look her.

And so they questioned the girl
Along with many more.
To learn if she did money get
And what xactly was the score?
Who having finished their intent
They visited the spot
And said twas done with full consent
Of the fair HOTTENTOT.

When speaking free from all alarm
The whole she does deride
And says she thinks there is no great harm
In showing her backside.

And now good people let us go
To see this wondrous sight
We'll have uh gawk, toss her uh sweet
Such recreation cant be beat
Lets not be critical of what Loves got
Cause lookin at her past-tense end
Delights so much the HOTTENTOT.

(The Chorus is now The Chorus of the Court.)

Scene 20B
The Venus Hottentot Before the Law (Continued)
(Historical Extract)

THE CHORUS OF THE COURT.
We representatives of the Law
have hauled into Court the case
of a most unfortunate female, who has been known to exhibit
   herself
to the view of the Public
in a manner offensive to decency and disgraceful to our
   country.
This Court wonders if she is at inny time
under the countrol of others, or some dark force, some say,
   black magic
making her exhibition against her will.
We ask 2 questions: is she or was she ever indecent? And at
   inny time held against her will?
We do not wish to send her adrift in the world without
   asylum of a friend
a friend ready to receive and protect her.
But to the honour and credit of this country,
she will not find herslf without friends and protection
even if she may be employed to expose herself
in a most disgraceful manner, however,
the Court intends to interfere and
receive her immediately under its protection;
for the purpose of restoring her to her own friends and her
   own country
so that she not become a burden to the state and contribute
   to our growing social ills.
(Rest.)
Lets get this show on the road.

We begin with a writ of *Habeas Corpus.*

Scene 20C
The Venus Hottentot Before the Law (Continued)
(Dictionary Extract)
From Websters Ninth New Collegiate Dictionary, page 545

Apart from the "courtroom" The Venus sits in a jail cell.

THE VENUS.
(Rest.)
Habeas Corpus: Literally: "you should have the body" for
submitting.
(Rest.)
They don't want me in their country. But to go home now
would be disgraceful.

Scene 20D
The Venus Hottentot Before the Law (Continued)
First Witness

THE CHORUS OF THE COURT.
First Witness!

THE CHORUS LEADER.
We call for the testimony of her present Keeper
One called "THE MOTHER-SHOWMAN."
Mother-Showman, take the stand!

THE MOTHER-SHOWMAN.
The one called Mother-Showman is
unavailable for comment.

THE CHORUS OF THE COURT.
Where is she? Find her!

74

THE MOTHER-SHOWMAN.
Shes got 9 ugly mouths to feed.
She works day in day out, folks.
As to any questions
concerning the Goddess Venus H.
If Mothers been unkind she swears to mend her evil ways!

THE CHORUS OF THE COURT.
Haul her in here!

THE MOTHER-SHOWMAN.
Mama submits
A certificate of baptism of the so-called Venus Hottentot
As proof that I take good care of her.

THE CHORUS LEADER.
Hmmmmmm. Interesting.
Submit the certificate of baptism as Exhibit A.

Scene 20E
The Venus Hottentot Before the Law (Continued)
(Historical Extract – Exhibit A)

THE NEGRO RESURRECTIONIST.
Exhibit A: The Certificate of Baptism

THE VENUS.
(Rest.)
Baptised. 1 December 1811. The ceremony took place in
Manchester, the clergyman being Reverand Joshua Brookes.
The certificate of baptism is preserved in Paris. It states:

"December 1. Sarah Bartmaan a Female Hottentot from the
Colony of the Cape of Good Hope, born on the Borders of
Caffraria, baptized this Day by Permission of the Lord
Bishop."

Scene 20F
The Venus Hottentot Before the Law (Continued)
Witness 1 and Witness 2

THE CHORUS OF THE COURT.
Lets get uh witness on the stand!

(The Chorus ejects one of its members: Witness #1.)

THE NEGRO RESURRECTIONIST.
1st Witness:
Historical Extract: From a Mr. Hall, Member of Society

WITNESS #1.
I saw her, oh several times.
Call me and my Mrs. her regulars. She was always
Standing on a stage 2 feet high, clothed in a light dress,
A dress thuh color of her own skin.
She looked, well, naked, kin I say that?
The whole place smelled of shit.
She didnt speak at all.
My Mrs. always fainted.

*(The Chorus ejects another member: Witness #2. Witness #1 rejoins
The Chorus.)*

THE CHORUS OF THE COURT.
Whos next?! Whos next!?

THE NEGRO RESURRECTIONIST.
2nd Witness:
Historical Extract: Mr. Charles Mathews visited The Venus and
related this scene to his now widow:

WITNESS #2.
Im a widow.

THE CHORUS OF THE COURT.
Widow, tell us whatcha seen.

WITNESS #2.
I saw nothin.
Hearsay only.
2nd hand.

THE CHORUS OF THE COURT.
Thatll do.
Spit it out.

WITNESS #2.
Good people, Im uh Widow.
My dear man was fond of sights and before he died
he viewd The Venus H.
He related it to me this way:
"She was surrounded by many persons, some *females!*
One pinched her, another walked round her;
one gentleman *poked* her with his cane;
Uh *lady* used her parasol to see if all was, as she called it,
     '*natural.*'
Through all of this the creature didnt speak.
Maybe uh sigh or 2 maybe when she seemed inclined to
     protest the pawing."
She once handed my man a feather from her head.
Theyre said to bring good luck.
"A fight ensued. 3 men died. Uh little boy went mad. Uh
woman lost her child."
My man escaped with thuh feather intact.
(Rest.)
But thuh shock of her killed him, I think,
cause 2 days later he was dead.
Ive thrown thuh feather away.

Scene 20G
The Venus Hottentot Before the Law (Continued)
Exhibit B

THE VENUS.
Exhibit B:
A feather from the head of the
so-called Venus H.
The feathers were said to bring good luck —
when stroked such feathers cured infertility.
When ground and ingested these same feathers proved
a brilliant aphrodisiac.

Scene 20H
The Venus Hottentot Before the Law (Continued)
Witness 3 and Witness 4

THE CHORUS LEADER.
Let the Widow step down.
Who's next? Who's next?

THE CHORUS OF THE COURT.
We call to the stand
the man who watches her from afar:
the Baron Docteur.

THE BARON DOCTEUR.
The Baron Docteur is
unavailable for comment.

THE CHORUS OF THE COURT.
Outrage! ItsanOutrage!

THE BARON DOCTEUR.
Im speaking on The Venus subject at a conference.
Yll have to wait till then.

THE CHORUS OF THE COURT.
Outrage! ItsanOutrage!
Lets get someone anyone on the stand!

(They eject another member. Witness #3.)

THE CHORUS LEADER.
We call to the stand
a noted Abolitionist.

WITNESS #3.
I am a noted abolitionist.

THE NEGRO RESURRECTIONIST.
Historical Extract Category: Journalistic:
A letter of protest appearing in *Morning Chronicle, Friday 12
Oct. 1810*

WITNESS #3.
"Sir, As a friend to liberty, in every situation of life, I cannot
help calling your attention to a subject, which I am sure
needs only be noticed by you to insure your immediate
observation and comment. I allude to that wretched object
advertised and publicly shown for money — the "Hottentot
Venus" who has been brought here as a subject for the
curiosity of this country, for 2 cents a-head. Her keeper is the
only gainer. I am no advocate of these sights, on the contrary,
I think it base in the extreme, that *any* human beings should
be thus exposed!"

WITNESS #4.
Equal time! Equal time!
I represent a man who knows!

THE NEGRO RESURRECTIONIST.
A reply appearing in *The Morning Chronicle, 23 Oct. 1810.*

WITNESS #4.
"Since the English last took possession of the colonies, we
have been consitstantly solicited to bring to this country,
subjects well worthy of the attention of the Virtuoso, and the
curious in general. And pray, has she not as good a right to
exhibit herself as the Famous Irish Giant or the renouned
Dogfaced Dancing Dwarf?!?!"

THE CHORUS OF THE COURT.
Thank you, Sirs.
You may step down.
The court grants the writ of *Habeas Corpus.*
Bring up the body of this female.

Scene 20I
The Venus Hottentot Before the Law (Continued)
(Historical Extract)

The Venus comes out of her cage.

THE CHORUS OF THE COURT.
We call The Venus Hottentot.

THE VENUS.
Im called Venus Hottentot.

THE CHORUS OF THE COURT.
She speaks!!
(Rest.)
Simple questions first.
Who are you?
Where are you from?

Any family?
Are you happy?
Are you a witch?
Were you ever beaten?
Did you like it was it good?
Do you wanna go home?
If so, when?! If so, when?!
Answer, come on, spit it out!

THE VENUS.
THE VENUS.
THE VENUS.

THE VENUS.
The Venus Hottentot
is unavailable for comment.

THE CHORUS OF THE COURT.
Dont push us, Girl!
We could lock you up for life!
Answer this:
Are you here of yr own free will
or are you under some restraint?

THE VENUS.
Im here to make a mint.

THE CHORUS OF THE COURT.
Hubba-Hubba-Hubba-Hubba.
(Order-order-order-order.)

THE VENUS.
After all Ive gone through so far
to go home penniless would be disgraceful.

THE CHORUS OF THE COURT.
Is poverty more disgraceful than nakedness?
We think not!

THE CHORUS LEADER.
Shut her down!
Send her home!

THE VENUS.
Good people. Let me stay.

THE CHORUS LEADER.
No way!
Her kind bear Gods bad mark and, baptised or not,
They blacken-up the honor of our fair country.
Get her out of here!

THE CHORUS OF THE COURT.
Shut her down!
Send her home!

THE VENUS.
No!
Please. Good good honest people.
If I bear thuh bad mark what better way to cleanse it off?
Showing my sinful person as a caution to you all could,
in the Lords eyes
be a sort of
repentance
and I could wash off my dark mark.
I came here black.
Give me the chance to leave here white.

THE CHORUS OF THE COURT.
Hmmmmmmmmmmm.
Her words strike a deep chord.
(Rest.)
One more question, Girl, uh:
Have you ever been indecent?

THE CHORUS OF THE COURT.
THE VENUS.
THE CHORUS OF THE COURT.

THE VENUS.
(Rest.)
"Indecent?"

THE CHORUS OF THE COURT.
Nasty.

THE VENUS.
Never.
No. I am just me.

THE CHORUS OF THE COURT.
Whats that supposed to mean?!?!

THE VENUS.
To hide yr shame is evil.
I show mine. Would you like to see?

THE CHORUS OF THE COURT.
Outrage! Ssanoutrage!
Outrage! Ssanoutrage!
(Order order order order.)
(Order order order order.)
God! Weve got
a lot to think about.
Recess! Recess!
Lets take a break.

(They huddle in a knot.)

THE NEGRO RESURRECTIONIST.
The year was 1810, three years after the Bill for the Abolition
of the Slave-Trade had been passed in Parliament. Among

protests and denials, horror and fascination the show went
on.
(Rest.)

Scene 20J:

Scene 20J
The Venus Hottentot Before the Law (Continued)
(Historical Extract)

THE CHORUS OF THE COURT.
Hear ye hear ye hear
All rise and hear our ruling:
It appears to The Court
that the person on whose behalf this suit was brought
lives under no restraint.
Her exhibition sounds indecent
but look at her now, shes nicely dressed.
It is clear shes got grand plots and plans
to make her mark and her mint by playing outside the
    bounds so that we find
Her person much depraved but she sez her show is part of
    Gods great plan
and we buy that.
Besides she has the right to make her mark just like the
    Dancing Irish Dwarf
and she seems well fed.
At this time the Court rules
Not to rule.
(Rest.)
In closing, whatever happens to her
we should note that
it is very much to the credit of our great country
that even a female Hottentot can find a court to review her
    status.

(Rest.)
(Rest.)
HAHAHAHAHAHAHAHAHAHHAHAHAHAHHAHAHA
HAHAHAHAHAHAHAHAHAHAHAHAHAHAHHAHAHHAHAHA

THE BARON DOCTEUR.
Order! Order!
Order! Order!

(The Chorus vanishes.)

THE NEGRO RESURRECTIONIST.
Scene 19:
A Scene of Love
(?)

Scene 19
A Scene of Love (?)

THE VENUS.
THE BARON DOCTEUR.
THE VENUS.
THE BARON DOCTEUR.
THE VENUS.
THE BARON DOCTEUR.
THE VENUS.
THE BARON DOCTEUR.
THE VENUS.

Scene 18
She Always Was My Favorite Child

THE BARON DOCTEUR.
You show The Venus Hottentot?

THE MOTHER-SHOWMAN.
Thats right.
Thought up her name and everything.
Im always by her side.

THE BARON DOCTEUR.
I'd like to take her off yr hands.

THE MOTHER-SHOWMAN.
You would, huh?
To what purpose?

THE BARON DOCTEUR.
Thats none of yr business.

THE MOTHER-SHOWMAN.
You want her for a servant, right?
Shes got talents but not on that line.
Besides. Shes wild. Pure heathen.
May revert as they call it inny minute.
Bite you square in thuh face.
My ears thuh proof of that.
Shes no servin girl, Sir. Sorry.

THE BARON DOCTEUR.
Im a doctor.

THE MOTHER-SHOWMAN.
Shes my prize Doc.

THE BARON DOCTEUR.
She must be a handful
to maintain.

THE MOTHER-SHOWMAN.
That she is.

THE BARON DOCTEUR.
Her appeal wont last much longer.
The crowds are looking skimpy.

THE MOTHER-SHOWMAN.
Thats my business.

THE BARON DOCTEUR.
Come on. How much.

THE MOTHER-SHOWMAN.
Long term
or short term rental?

THE BARON DOCTEUR.
Permanent.
Name yr price.

THE MOTHER-SHOWMAN.
THE MOTHER-SHOWMAN.

THE MOTHER-SHOWMAN.
I might retire afterall.
What do you want her for?

THE BARON DOCTEUR.
Thats not yr concern.
How much?

THE MOTHER-SHOWMAN.
THE BARON DOCTEUR.

THE BARON DOCTEUR.
Ive watched you with her, woman.
You kick her like I kick my dog!

THE MOTHER-SHOWMAN.
THE BARON DOCTEUR.

THE MOTHER-SHOWMAN.
THE BARON DOCTEUR.

(Rest.)

THE MOTHER-SHOWMAN.
We seem to have an understanding.

THE BARON DOCTEUR.
How much.

THE MOTHER-SHOWMAN.
A lot.

THE BARON DOCTEUR.
Ok.

THE MOTHER-SHOWMAN.
A ton.

THE BARON DOCTEUR.
All right.

THE MOTHER-SHOWMAN.
A mint!
A fortune!
Fort Knox!

THE BARON DOCTEUR.
Here here take it take it.

THE MOTHER-SHOWMAN.
My retirement!
(Rest.)
Whatll you do with her? Im curious.

THE BARON DOCTEUR.
Get her out of that filthy cage for one.
Teach her French. Who knows.

THE MOTHER-SHOWMAN.
Be good to her, Sir.
We sure will miss her.
She always was my favorite child.

Scene 17
You Look Like You Need a Vacation

THE NEGRO RESURRECTIONIST.
Scene 17:

THE CHORUS OF 8 HUMAN WONDERS.
Ive been in this line of work for years and years
and every time the crowds gather
and the lights flash on me
I freak out.
That girl they call The Venus, The Venus Hottentot, shes
    holding up, well,
pretty well: stupendous. Stupendous. Still:
Shes got that faraway look in her eye.
That look of someone who dont know whats in store.
She signed on for 2 years. "One more month" shes thinking
"One more month one more month one more month."
But should I tell her? No, I havent got the balls to say:
Lovely Venus, with yr looks theres absolutely no escape.

THE VENUS.
Whos there.

THE BARON DOCTEUR.
A friend.
Im yr biggest fan.

THE VENUS.
No —

THE BARON DOCTEUR.
I find you fascinating

THE VENUS.
No —

THE BARON DOCTEUR.
Not like that, Girl.
Im a doctor.
"Doctor."
Understand?

THE VENUS.
THE BARON DOCTEUR.

(Rest.)

THE VENUS.
I understand.

THE BARON DOCTEUR.
Ive brought you chockluts. Here.
You like?

(He gives her a red heart box of chocolates.)

THE VENUS.
I like.

THE BARON DOCTEUR.
Well.
Lets have a look.
Stand still stand still, sweetheart
I'll orbit.

Dont start Ive doctors eyes and hands.
Well.
Extraordinary.
(Rest.)
(Rest.)
Sweetheart, how would you like to go to Paris?

THE VENUS.
"Paris." Well.
"Paris."
Whats that?

THE BARON DOCTEUR.
A big town!
Only a short boat ride away!

THE VENUS.
"Paris."

THE BARON DOCTEUR.
"The City of Lights!"
I'd teach you French.

THE VENUS.
"French."

THE BARON DOCTEUR.
Ive paid yr Mother off.
Yd have a clean room.
Mix with my associates.
Move in a better circle.

THE VENUS.
"Circle."
(Rest.)
Yr hands. Theyre clean.
Are you rich?

THE BARON DOCTEUR.
Very.

THE VENUS.
I like rich.

THE BARON DOCTEUR.
Its settled then.
I find you quite phenomenal.
Hell, you look like you need a vacation. Say "yes!"
Say "yes" and we'll leave this minute.

THE VENUS.
Do I have a choice?

THE BARON DOCTEUR.
Yes. God. Of course.

THE VENUS.
Will you pay me?

THE BARON DOCTEUR.
I could pay you, yes.

THE VENUS.
100 a week.

THE BARON DOCTEUR.
Deal.

THE VENUS.
New clothes and good meals.

THE BARON DOCTEUR.
Whatever you want.

THE VENUS.
My own room.

THE BARON DOCTEUR.
(Rest.)
Yll sleep with me.
Say "yes."

THE VENUS.
THE BARON DOCTEUR.

THE BARON DOCTEUR.
Think it over. I'll stand by.

THE VENUS.
THE BARON DOCTEUR.

(Rest.)

(The Baron Docteur stands out of sight to let her think it over. Enter The Mother-Showman. She rattles a stick along the bars of the cage.)

THE MOTHER-SHOWMAN.
Not gond yet?! Shit.
I guess he changed his mind.
He'll be back inny minute wanting his money
and if I dont fork it over he'll gun me down most likely
    Christ!
What a business this is.
9 ugly mouths to feed plus my own.
Hup Ho, Girl! Wake up!
We got a crowd out there.

THE VENUS.
(yes.)

THE MOTHER-SHOWMAN.
Theyre fresh from the pubs and I hate to say it
but the stench of liquor on their collective breaths

THE VENUS.
(yes.)

THE MOTHER-SHOWMAN.
is only matched by
the stench of yr shit in this pen, Girl! Jesus!

THE VENUS.
(yes.)

THE MOTHER-SHOWMAN.
Jesus! *Yr an animal!*

THE VENUS.
Yes.

THE BARON DOCTEUR.
Come on then get up.
Lets get going.

THE VENUS.
Yes.

THE BARON DOCTEUR.
Paris! Paris! Paris! HO!

THE VENUS.
Yes.

THE NEGRO RESURRECTIONIST.
Scene 16:
The Intermission:

INTERMISSION

Scene 16
Several Years From Now:
In The Anatomical Theatre of Tübingen:
The Dis(-re-)memberment of The Venus Hottentot,
Part I

Scene 16 runs during intermission. House lights should come up and the audience should be encouraged to walk out of the theatre, take their intermission break, and then return.

The Baron Docteur at a podium. He reads from his notebook. The Bride-To-Be sits off to the side reading from her love letters.

THE BRIDE-TO-BE.
"My love for you, My Love, is artificial,
Fabricated much like this epistle."

THE BARON DOCTEUR.
The height, measured after death,
was 4 feet 11 and 1/2 inches.
The total weight of the body was 98 pounds *avoirdupois*.
As aside I should say
That as to the *value* of the informations that I present
to you today there can be no doubt.
Their significance will be felt far beyond our select
community. All that in mind
I understand that my yield is
long in length
And while my finds are complete compensation
for the amount of labor expended upon them
I do invite you, Distinguished Gentlemen,
Collegues and yr Distinguished Guests,
if you need *relief*

Please take yourselves uh breather in thuh lobby.
My voice will surely carry beyond these walls and if not
my finds are published. Forthcoming in *The Royal College
Journal of Anatomy.*
Merely as an aside, Gentlemen.
(Rest.)

THE NEGRO RESURRECTIONIST.
Scene 16:
Several years from Now:
In the Anatomical Theatre of Tübingen:
The Dis(-re-)memberment of The Venus Hottentot, Part I:

THE BRIDE-TO-BE.
"My Love for you, My Love, is artificial
Fabricated much like this epistle."

THE BARON DOCTEUR.
The height, measured after death,
was 4 feet 11 and 1/2 inches.
The total weight of the body was 98 pounds *avoirdupois.*
In the following notes my attention is chiefly directed
to the more perishable soft structures of the body.
The skeleton will form the subject of future examination.
(Rest.)
External Characteristics:
The great amounts of subcutaneous fat were
quite surprising. On the front of the thigh for instance
fat measured 1 inch in thickness.
On the thighs reverse the measure of fat was
4 inches deep.
On the buttocks proper, rested the fatty cushion, a.k.a.
Steatopygia the details of which I'll relate in due course.
(Rest.)
The Skin:
Prevaling color: orange-brown tolerably uniform in tint
on all parts of the body save on abdomen and thighs:
2 shades darker.

(Rest.)

The palms of the hands
and soles of the feet
were almost white.

(Rest.)

The Face:

Remarkable for its great breadth and flatness
Presenting to me resemblances to Mongolian and Simian
(previously noted by several other scholars).

The faces outline: both pecular and characteristic
being broad in the *malar* region
Contracting above the forehead but tapering suddenly
to form a narrow chin.

The great space between the eyes was 1.8: remarkable.
The eyelids horizontal apertures were a full .95.
Irises dark-brown with olive-brown *conjunctiva.*

In profile the nose was nearly straight, straight on it was
    broad
and much depressed.

One and a half across the base and but one-half inch
one-half inch from tip to *septum.*

Nostrils, Gentlemen, were patulous,
of regular oval form: .5 in length, .3 in breadth
Septum narium short and broad.

Aperture of mouth: 1.7 inch in width
With lips
broad and overted especially the upper one.

Chin was flat and angularish
Ear 2.3 in its vertical diameter
The lobe quite underdeveloped.

(Rest.)

The Hair on the scalp was black.
Arranged in numerous separate tufts
each tuft composed of a bunch of spirally-
curled hairs. Much interwoven.

The length of the tufts atop the head were from one inch to
    1.5.

Becoming shorter and smaller at the scalps edge.
Several of the individual hairs when pulled out straight
Were found to measure a full 7 inches.
On the scalp were several spots completely bald:
The subject when alive wore wigs which
could have produced the bare patches.
(A warning, Gentlemen, to us all.)
Eyebrows were very scanty.
Eyelashes short: .2 inch hairs.
On the *pubes* and *labia majora*
A few small scattered tufts
Of crisply-curled black hairs were present.
When pulled out straight these stretched out
over 3 inches long.
(Rest.)
(Rest.)

THE BRIDE-TO-BE.
"My Love for you, My Love, is artificial
Fabricated much like this epistle
Constructed with mans finest powrs
Will last through the days and the years and the hours."
(Rest.)

THE BARON DOCTEUR.
The *Mammae,* situated exactly
Over the fourth and fifth ribs,
Were a full 6 inches apart at the inner edge of their bases.
They were soft
Soft, flaccid and subpendulous:
4 inches in diameter at the base
and about the same from base to apex.
Nipple very prominent of blackish-brownish hue
and 1 inch in diameter. An areola
darker than the neighbor skin
extended around for 1 and 1/2 inches
from the nipples centre.

(Rest.)
What remains of the external characters, the information,
perhaps, of greatest interest,
Will be revealed toward the end of my presentation
Under the head of *Generative or Reproductive Organs.*
(Rest.)
The Muscular System:
(Rest.)

THE BRIDE-TO-BE.
"Not to a rose not to a pansy not to daffodil
Compares my Love, My Love, which will Stretch back"
(Rest.)

THE BARON DOCTEUR.
Presenting here, in the interest of time,
only those special points of interest.
You look, Distinguished Collegue, as if you need relief
Or sleep.
Please, Sir, indulge yourself. Go take uh break.
Ive got strong lungs:
So please, if you need air, excuse yrself.
Youll hear me in the hallway.
Uh hehm:
The *Depressor anguli oris* and the *Depressor labii inferioris,*
that is, the muscles of the mouth, were both unusually
well developed, the latter
forming a distinct prominence causing
that protuberant under lip
so characteristic of the Negro tribe.
Our Anthropological scholars present will remember that
although, while during her stay with us, she picked up
uh bit of English, French and even Dutch all *patios,*
the native language of this woman is said
to have consisted entirely
of an almost uninterrupted succession
of clicks and explosives.
(Rest.)

A language of *clicks*, Gentlemen.
(Rest.)
The attachment of these mouth muscles were as usual.
Ear muscles, that is *Retrahens aurem*,
were only moderately developed. They arose
by 2 slips from the base and middle of the *Mastoid Process*
and had the usual insertion.
The *Attollens* and *Attrahens Aurem*
were injured in removing the *Calvarium*.
The *Sternomastoid,*
muscles of the front of the neck and the muscles of the
abdomen
were distinct in their attachments.
The former arose by a long and slender tendon the latter
by muscular fibres from the inner end of the clavicle
breadth measured 1.7 inches. The *omo-hyoid* muscle presented
a peculaiarity on both sides having no origin from the
Scapula.
Its inferior extremity spread out to form a somewhat
widened attachment to the *Clavicle* —
about an inch from the outer end and behind the *Trapezius.*
In the muscles of the back of the neck and trunk
there was no trace of any fibers continued from the
normal *Latissimus dorsi* to represent
the *Dorso-epitrochlear* of the lower mammalia.
(Rest.)
The *Levator anguli scapulae* arose from the posterior *Tubercles*
of the 1st, 2nd and 4th cervical vertebrae
and had the usual insertion but with an addition:
a small slip which passed downwards
to the middle of the *Serratus magnus.*
This small slip may be an indication of the *Levator claviculae*
as noted by Dr. McWhinnie and now well known to all
anatomists,
though the name was first recognised in human myology
by Dr. Wood. The *Splenius colli*
was inserted by a double tendon into the *Transverse Process*

of the 2 upper cervical vertabrae, the lower tendon
being somewhat larger. The *Cerviccelis Ascendens* was
distinctly separate from the *Scrolumbalis.*
It arose by delicate tendons from the posterior angles
of the 1st, 2nd, 3rd and 4th ribs
which joined in a muscular belly sending off similar slips
to the *Transverse Process* of the 6th and 7th
hhhh *Cervical Vertebrae.*
The *Trachelo-mastoid* was divided into two portions ...
thin delicate and membranous sprung by delicate
delicate tendons from the transverse process of
the 4th and 1st dorsal ...
The occipital group of muscles were
all strongly developed ...
As for the Triceps, the 2 usual *Humeral Origins* were fused
into a single head
which reached as high as the insertion of the *Teres Minor.*
Scapular origin normal.
(Rest.)
The tendon of the *Extensor minimi digiti* in the right hand
divided above the annular ligament
into 2 distinct tendons
which passed under the ligament in separate grooves
and, proceeding over the *Metacarpo-phalangeal* articulation,
were re-united, and joining
with the tendon of the *Extensor cummunis digitorum* formed
the tendinous expansion upon the *dorsum* of the 5th digit.
In the left hand the tendon was also split, but
the 2 divisions
(Rest.)
passed through the same groove.

THE BRIDE-TO-BE.
"Not to a rose not to a pansy not to daffodil
Compares my Love, My Love, which will
Stretch back and forth reach all through all Time
Deep from my heart, to pri-mordial slime."

THE BARON DOCTEUR.

The *Extensor primi internodii pollicis*
was normal in its development and attachments.
(Rest.)
On removing the *fascia* from the superior border
of the *Gluteus maximus* a considerable portion of the
Gluteus medius was exposed.
The condition of the *flexor brevis digitorum pedis* presented
rather anomalous characters
it might be said to form 2 dististinct muscles.
This condition interests us
because of the well known fact that in the chimpanzee,
and all inferior Primates, a considerable portion of this
 muscle
always arises from the long *flexor* tendon while in man alone
the whole of it commonly takes orgin from the *Os calcis.*
(An arrangement recently described by Dr. Wood.)
The relation of the arrangements of the muscular system of
 Man
to that of the inferior Primates as we know
was first clearly described by Dr. Huxley
in his Hunterian Lectures
delivered at the Royal College of Surgeons earlier this year.
unfortunately only a brief abstract has hitherto been
 published.
Her shoulders back and chest had grace.
Her charming hands... *uh hehm.*
Where was I?
Oh, of course:
On referring to the absolutely different characters
— there laid down
we find that in no case does our subject
pass over the boundary line.
(Rest.)
Thank you.

(He exits.)

[INTERMISSION CONTINUED

Historical Extract: Musical

Wonder #7 sings a song.

WONDER #7.
A Song on behalf of myself and The Hottentot Venus, to the
Ladies of New York:

"Fair" Ladies, Ive saild, in obedience to you
From NEW YORK, since the last Masquerade, to PERU
There, to gaurd gainst all possible scandal tonight
I turnd Priest and have conjurd my Black-a-moor white.
A strange Metamorphosis! — Who that had seen us
Tother night, would take this for *The Hottentot Venus*
Or me for poor Jack? Now Im Priest of the Sun
And she, a queer kind of Peruvian Nun.
Though in this our Novitiate, we *preach* but so, so
Youll grant that at least we *appear* comme il faut.
In pure Virgin robes, full of fears and alarms
How demurely she veils her protuberant charms!
Thus oft, to atone for absurdities past
Tom Foll turns a Methodist Preacher at last.
Yet the *Critics* not *we* were to blame — For od rot em
There was nothing but innocent fun *at the bottom!*

(Wonder #7 exits.)]

END OF INTERMISSION

Scene 15
Counting Down

THE NEGRO RESURRECTIONIST.
31
30
29
28
27
26
25
24
23
22
21
20
19
18
17
16
15
14
(Rest.)
Scene 14:

Scene 14
In the Orbital Path of The Baron Docteur

The lovers in bed.

THE BARON DOCTEUR.
Quatorze
Treize
Douze

Onze
Dix
Neuf
Huit
Sept
Six
Cinq
Quatre
Trois
Deux
Un
(Rest.)
It's dark in here. Spooky.
Lets have light.

THE VENUS.
Keep it dark.
Are yr eyes closed?

THE BARON DOCTEUR.
Theyre closed.
Hurry up. Im eager.

THE NEGRO RESURRECTIONIST.
Scene #14:
In the Orbital Path of the Baron Docteur:

THE VENUS.
Voilà. Open yr eyes.

THE BARON DOCTEUR.
THE VENUS.

THE BARON DOCTEUR.
Too dark to see.
Lie here beside me, Sweetheart.
Mmmm. Thats good.

THE VENUS.
Love me?

THE BARON DOCTEUR.
I do.
Ah, this is the life.
(He recites a poem.)
"My love for you is artificial.
Fabricated much like this epistle.
Its crafted with my finest powers
To last through the days and the weeks and the hours."
(Rest.)
I made it up myself
Just this morning.
You like it?

THE VENUS.
Mmmmmmm.

THE VENUS.
THE BARON DOCTEUR.

(Rest.)

THE BARON DOCTEUR.
You know what I want more than anything?

THE VENUS.
Me.
Lets have some love.

THE BARON DOCTEUR.
After you. Guess what I want.

THE VENUS.
More me.
Kiss?

THE BARON DOCTEUR.
Im an everyday anatomist.
One in a crowd of millions.

THE VENUS.
Another kiss.
Mmmm thats good.
Sweetheart, lie back down.

THE BARON DOCTEUR.
You were just yrself and crowds came running.
I was fascinated and a little envious but just a little.
A doctor cant just be himself
no onell pay a cent for that.
Imagine me just being me.

THE VENUS.
Hahahahahahaha

THE BARON DOCTEUR.
What a strange laugh.

THE VENUS.
Lie back down.
Hold me close to you. Its cold.
Love me?

THE BARON DOCTEUR.
I do.

THE VENUS.
THE BARON DOCTEUR.
THE VENUS.

(Rest.)

THE BARON DOCTEUR.
Most great minds discover something.

Ive had ideas for things but.
My ideas r —
(You wouldnt understand em anyway.)

THE VENUS.
Touch me
down here.

THE BARON DOCTEUR.
In you, Sweetheart Ive met my opposite-exact.
Now if I could only match you.

THE VENUS.
That feels good.
Now touch me here.

THE BARON DOCTEUR.
Crowds of people screamd yr name! "Venus Hottentot!!"
You were a sensation! I wouldnt mind a bit of that.
Known. Like you!
Only, of course, in my specific circle.

THE VENUS.
You could be whatshisname: Columbus.

THE BARON DOCTEUR.
Thats been done.

THE VENUS.
Columbus II?

THE BARON DOCTEUR.
Dont laugh at me.

(Rest.)

THE VENUS.
THE BARON DOCTEUR.
THE VENUS.

(Rest.)

THE BARON DOCTEUR.
Here. Yr favorite: chockluts. Have some.

(The Baron Docteur turns his back to her.)

THE VENUS.
Petis Coeurs
Rhum Caramel
Pharaon
Bouchon Fraise
Escargot Lait
Enfant de Bruxelles.
(Rest.)
Do you think I look like
one of these little chocolate brussels infants?

THE BARON DOCTEUR.
You cant stay here forever you know.

THE VENUS.
Capezzoli di Venere.
The nipples of Venus. Mmmmm. My favorite.

THE BARON DOCTEUR.
Ive got a wife. Youve got a homeland and a family back there.

THE VENUS.
I dont wanna go back inny more.
I like yr company too much.
Besides, it was a shitty life.
(Rest.)
Whatre you doing?

THE BARON DOCTEUR.
Nothing.

THE VENUS.
Lemmie see.

THE BARON DOCTEUR.
Dont look! Dont look at me.
Look off
somewhere
Eat yr chockluts.
eat em slow.
Touch yrself.
Good.
Good.

(He's masturbating. He has his back to her. He sneaks little looks at her over his shoulder. He cumms.)

THE VENUS.
Whyd you do that?

THE BARON DOCTEUR.
Im polite.

(Rest.)

THE VENUS.
Love me?

THE BARON DOCTEUR.
Do I ever.

THE VENUS.
More than yr wife?

THE BARON DOCTEUR.
More than my life.
And my wife.
She and I are childless you know.

THE VENUS.
I know.
These are yummy.
(Rest.)
Wear this uhround yr neck and never take it off.
Its uh good luck feather. Uh sort of amulet.
It might help.

THE BARON DOCTEUR.
It smells of you.

THE VENUS.
Love me?

THE BARON DOCTEUR.
Yes.
You dont want to go home?

THE VENUS.
Not inny more.
(Rest.)
Love me?

THE BARON DOCTEUR.
I do.

THE VENUS.
Lie down.
And kiss me.
Here.
And here.
And here.
And here.

And here, you missed a spot.
Dearheart.

THE BARON DOCTEUR.
Dearheart.

THE VENUS.
You could discover *me*.

THE BARON DOCTEUR.
THE VENUS.
THE BARON DOCTEUR.

(Rest.)

THE BARON DOCTEUR.
THE VENUS.
THE BARON DOCTEUR.

(Rest.)

THE BARON DOCTEUR.
I love you, Girl.

THE VENUS.
Lights out.

Scene 13
Footnote #7

The Negro Resurrectionist reads from The Baron Docteur's notebook.

THE NEGRO RESURRECTIONIST.
Footnote #7
Historical Extract: Category: Medical:

(Rest.)

A DETAILED PHYSICAL DESCRIPTION OF THE SO-CALLED VENUS HOTTENTOT

(Rest.)

"Her hair was black and wooly, much like that of the common Negro, the slits of the eyes horizontal as in Mongols, not oblique; the brows straight, wide apart and very much flattened close to the top of the nose, but jutting out at the temple above the cheekbones; her eyes were dark and lively; her lips blackish, terribly thick; her complexion very dark."

(Rest.)

"Her ears were much like those found in monkeys: Small, weakly formed at the *tragus,* and vanishing behind almost completely."

(Rest.)

"Her breasts she usually lifted and tightened beneath the middle part of her dress, but, left free, they hung bulkily and terminated obliquely in a blackish areola about 1 and ½ inches in diameter pitted with radiating wrinkles, near the center of what was a nipple so flattened and obliterated as to be barely visible: The color of her skin was on the whole a yellowish brown, almost as dark as her face."

(Rest.)

"Her movements had rapidity and came unexpected calling to mind well, with all respect to her, the movements of a monkey. Above all, she had a way of pushing out her lips just like the monkeys do. Her personality was sprightly, her memory good. She spoke low Dutch, tolerably good English — the men at the Academy and I tried to teach her French. She danced after the fashion of her own country and played with a fairly good ear upon a little instrument she called a Jew's Harp."

(Rest.)

"She had no body hair apart from a few short flecks of wool like that on her head, scattered about her pubic parts."

(Rest.)

"The wonders of her lower regions, will be fleshed out in greater detail at a later date."

(Rest.)
"This information was gleaned, as has been said, upon the
first and subsequent examinations which were performed in
the office of her personal physician. As stated for the record,
she submitted to these examinations as willingly as a patient
submits to his doctors eyes and hands."
(Rest.)
Scene #12:

Scene 12
Love Iduhnt What/She Used To Be

*The Venus stands alone. She's dressed in a beautiful dress
and looks fabulous.*

*The Chorus of Anatomists wanders in one by one. They get
to work.*

*The Baron Docteur wanders in. He watches. He wears his
feather amulet.*

ANATOMIST #8.
"The book is on the table!"

THE VENUS.
*Le livre est
sur la table!*

ANATOMIST #8.
"The book is on the floor!"

THE VENUS.
*Le livre est
par terre!*

ANATOMIST #8.
"And now the book is on my shoulder!"

114

THE VENUS.
Et maintenant, le livre est
sur mon épaule!

ANATOMIST #8.
"And now the book is on my head!"

THE VENUS.
Et maintenant, le livre est
sur ma tête!

(The Anatomists applaud most respectfully.)

ANATOMIST #8.
Thats excellent! And shes only been here
what, Sir, 6 months?

THE BARON DOCTEUR.
6 months thats right.

ANATOMIST #8.
Throws all of those throw-back theories back in the lake, I'd
     say.
Throw em back in the lake!

THE BARON DOCTEUR.
Not entirely, gentlemen.
We study a people as a group
and dont throw away our years of labor
because of one most glorious exception.

THE CHORUS OF ANATOMISTS.
hahahahahahahahahaha

(The Anatomists and The Baron Docteur laugh goodnaturedly. The
Venus joins in. While they laugh a new Anatomist wanders onstage.
He is The Baron Docteur's Grade-School Chum. He surreptitiously
hands The Baron Docteur a letter and wanders off.)

THE BARON DOCTEUR.
Enough play, gentlemen!
Lets get to work!

*(The Venus denudes. Perhaps 2 of the female Anatomists assist her.
Perhaps she is lightly clothed in a sheer fabric.)*

We'll start with simple figure drawing.
An important skill for any promising Anatomist.
(Rest.)
Sweetheart, stand here where the light is perfect on you.
Just relax.
Only doctors here.
Thats beautiful.
(Rest.)
Alright, gentlemen! Pose #1.

*(The Venus stands in profile. The Anatomists draw The Venus. The
Baron Docteur stands apart and reads his letter.)*

("Dear Sir:
I am a friend of yrs from way back.
Im sure you remember at least my face
we went to school together. How interesting
that we're both in the doctering business.
But no time for reminiscing, old friend,
I must cut straight to the point:
In yr liason with that Negress, Sir, you disgrace yrself.
Not to mention the pain yr causing yr sweet lovely wife.
A year in her bed is plenty, Sir. Surely yve tired of her
    heathen charms by now.
Send the Thing back where she came from
and return yrself to the boosom of yr senses.
Im speaking plain because as an old friend Ive
made it my responsiblilty to bring you back.
Sincerly yrs, A GRADE-SCHOOL CHUM.")
(Rest.)
(Rest.)

Gentlemen!
On to pose #2!
(Rest.)
Sweetheart, reverse profile, if you please.

*(The Venus stands in reverse profile. The Anatomists draw busily.
The Baron Docteur stands apart.)*

"Sincerely yrs, A GRADE-SCHOOL CHUM."
(Rest.)
(Rest.)
"I'm sure you remember at least my face."
(Rest.)
(Rest.)
"A GRADE-SCHOOL CHUM."
Ah, ridiculous!
"A GRADE-SCHOOL CHUM." Ha!
Just some busy eager beaver
Trying to beat my time, I'll bet.

(Rest.)
(Rest.)

THE VENUS.
THE BARON DOCTEUR.
THE VENUS.
THE BARON DOCTEUR.

(Rest.)

THE VENUS.
Love me?

THE BARON DOCTEUR.
How couldnt I?
Yr lovelier than ever.

THE VENUS.
THE BARON DOCTEUR.

(Rest.)
(Rest.)

THE BARON DOCTEUR.
Gentlemen!
Time to practice Measurements!

(The Anatomists measure The Venus. The Baron Docteur stands apart.)

From thuh vertex to thuh chin:

THE CHORUS OF 8 ANATOMISTS.
8.0 inches.

THE BARON DOCTEUR.
Vertex to
the top of shoulder in inches:

THE CHORUS OF 8 ANATOMISTS.
9.0.

THE BARON DOCTEUR.
To thuh upper part of thuh *sternum:*

THE CHORUS OF 8 ANATOMISTS.
10.5.

THE BARON DOCTEUR.
To thuh *formal cartlages* tip:

THE CHORUS OF 8 ANATOMISTS.
16.3.

THE BARON DOCTEUR.
To the *umbilicus:*

THE CHORUS OF 8 ANATOMISTS.
To the *umbilicus:*
23.5

THE BARON DOCTEUR.
To the *perinaeum:*

THE CHORUS OF 8 ANATOMISTS.
To the *perianeum:*
30.0

THE BARON DOCTEUR.
To the middle fingers tip
the arm being placed by the side:

THE CHORUS OF 8 ANATOMISTS.
32.2

THE BARON DOCTEUR.
To the middle fingers tip
the arm being extended from the side:

THE CHORUS OF 8 ANATOMISTS.
32.1

*(Again, The Grade-School Chum wanders in and surreptitiously
hands The Baron Docteur another letter. This time The Grade-School
Chum joins the group of measurers.)*

THE BARON DOCTEUR.
To the middle fingers tip
the arm being extended towards the viewer
full front:

THE CHORUS OF 8 ANATOMISTS.
32.1

THE BARON DOCTEUR.
To the lower edge
of the *patella:*

THE CHORUS OF 8 ANATOMISTS.
41.3.

THE BARON DOCTEUR.
To the sole of the foot:

THE CHORUS OF 8 ANATOMISTS.
To the sole of the foot:
55.9

(Rest.)

THE BARON DOCTEUR.
("Dear Sir, perhaps my first letter went unnoticed,
one scrap of paper
one among the several thousands littering yr desk and yr hot
    bed.")
(Rest.)
Transverse breadth of the head:

THE CHORUS OF 8 ANATOMISTS.
5.2

THE BARON DOCTEUR.
Transverse breadth of the shoulders:

THE CHORUS OF 8 ANATOMISTS.
12.0

THE BARON DOCTEUR.
("Another year has passed since I first wrote.
And although youve not married yr pet Hottentot
and play a good part with yr dear wife,")
(Rest.)
"(((I'd like to think its my note thats moved you to return
    home although
you reek of Hottentot-amour, Sir, and as a collegue its my
    duty to speak plain, Sir:
we all smell it!))"
(Rest.)
(Rest.)

(*The Anatomists sniff the air.*)

THE BARON DOCTEUR.
THE BARON DOCTEUR.
THE BARON DOCTEUR.
THE BARON DOCTEUR.

(*The Baron Docteur is lost in thought. The Anatomists wait patiently
for him to resume, then, turning their backs to The Venus, they steal
looks at her over their shoulders and jerk off [much like The Baron
Docteur did in Scene 14].*)

THE BARON DOCTEUR.
(Rest.)
Of the spine to the last lumbar vertebra?
(Rest.)
Circumference of the chest at the lower margin
of the 6th rib?
(Rest.)
Span of the arms when extended:
Pull em all the way out, Gentlemen!

THE GRADE-SCHOOL CHUM.
The measurements of her limb-bones
will of course

be corrected
after maceration, Sir?

THE BARON DOCTEUR.
THE GRADE-SCHOOL CHUM.

THE VENUS.
"Maceration?"

(Rest.)

THE NEGRO RESURRECTIONIST.
Footnote #8
Definition: Medical: *Maceration*
(Rest.)
"A process performed on the subject after the subjects death.
The subjects body parts are soaked in a chemical solution to
separate the flesh from the bones so that the bones may be
measured with greater accuracy."
(Rest.)

THE BARON DOCTEUR.
Thats enough for now.
Gentlemen:
Thats plenty for today and Im sure our lovely subjects
all exhausted.
Put yr hands together, Sirs.
Show Venus yr appreciation.

(They applaud politely.)

THE NEGRO RESURRECTIONIST.
Scene 11:
"For the Love of The Venus," Act II, Scene 12:

Scene 11
"For the Love of The Venus,"
Act II, Scene 12

*The Baron Docteur's chair is empty. The Negro Resurrection-
ist takes a seat and watches half-heartedly.*

THE BRIDE-TO-BE.
He sez he loves a Hottentot.

THE MOTHER.
Dont snuffle.

THE BRIDE-TO-BE.
A *Hottentot!*

THE MOTHER.
Blow yr nose.

THE BRIDE-TO-BE.
Hottentot Venus!

THE MOTHER.
Wipe yr eyes.
My sons lost his mind but
I have uh plan.
Listen up!
(Rest.)
His head has turned from yr bright sun.
He roams in thuh dark.
Let me speek plain:
He dudhnt love you inny more.

THE BRIDE-TO-BE.
Aaah me!

THE MOTHER.
[Uh multitude of responses are available.
Thuh antiquity response would be thuh Asp.
Get yrself uh poison-snake. Clasp it tuh yr boosom.
On thuh left side. Let it fill yr heart with death.
Cleopatra. Very moving. Old hat now though.
Thuh classical response would be tuh hang yrself.
Phaedra did that.
Elizabethan response would be tuh drown yrself.
A *la* little wassername.

THE BRIDE-TO-BE.
Ophelia.

THE MOTHER.
Good girl.
They also drank poison. Fell on their swords.
In modern dress they slit their wrists.
Fill their pockets with rocks.
Jump from bridges.
Infront of trains.
Sleeping pills. Take one or two too many. Thatll do it.
Hunger strike: turn yr face tuh thuh wall dont eat for weeks.
Thats like pining. But more dramatic.
To simply waste uhway ——.]
But none of that.
I have uh plan.
Get this:
Our young man wants uh Hottentot tuh love.
Uh Hottentot yr not, my dear.
But with some skill you can pretend.

THE BRIDE-TO-BE.
Pretend?

THE MOTHER.
Lets get to work.
I'll get that Uncle on our side.

We'll get you up, make you look wild
Get you up like a Hottentot.

THE BRIDE-TO-BE.
Like a Hottentot?

THE MOTHER.
And bring my son to his knees!
Lets get to work.

THE BRIDE-TO-BE.
Lets get to work.

(Curtain. The Chorus applauds.)

Scene 10
Footnote #9

THE NEGRO RESURRECTIONIST.
(Rest.)
Footnote #9
Historical Extract: Category: Medical:
(Rest.)
"The female Hottentot under my care has the usual falling off
of appearance common in women of 30 years old. Her
mammae are flaccid and elongated. While her *glutei* muscles
along with their coverings, the 2 prominent peculiar hemi-
spherical cushions of fat, are quite remarkable, more remarkable still are the long appendages which hang down from her
pudendum!"

*(The Baron Docteur snatches his notebook from The Negro
Resurrectionist's hands.)*

THE BARON DOCTEUR.
THE NEGRO RESURRECTIONIST.

Scene 9
Her Charming Hands/An Anatomical Columbus

The Venus sits in a chair wrapped up to her chin in a large cloth.

The Baron Docteur stands above her wielding a shiny and sharp pair of scissors.

He is giving her a haircut.

THE BARON DOCTEUR.
Hold still.
There now.
Open yr eyes and take a look.

THE VENUS.
Uh uhnn.

THE BARON DOCTEUR.
Its almost perfect.

THE VENUS.
Im nervous.
I could be bald.

THE BARON DOCTEUR.
Ive got the steadiest hands in the business.
Dearheart. Look.

THE VENUS.
Mmm.
Not bad.
A little uneven on the left.
Just there.

(He evens out her haircut.)

THE BARON DOCTEUR.
Did yr dresses come today?

THE VENUS.
They did.

THE BARON DOCTEUR.
Wear the yellow one tonite.

THE VENUS.
We're having company?

THE BARON DOCTEUR.
No.
Tonights dinner is just you and me.

THE VENUS.
Its always only you and me.
You and me this room that table.
We dont go out.
No one visits.
You dont want me seen.

THE BARON DOCTEUR.
Yr seen enough at the Academy.

THE VENUS.
That dont count.

THE BARON DOCTEUR.
We go for rides.

THE VENUS.
In a closed coach!

THE BARON DOCTEUR.
Ok Ok I confess:
I wanna keep my Sweets
all to myself.
Im very greedy.
(Rest.)
Take another look.

THE VENUS.
Looks all right.
Love me?

THE BARON DOCTEUR.
Mmm.

THE VENUS.
THE BARON DOCTEUR.

(Rest.)

THE BARON DOCTEUR.
Ok, up up!
Ive got some work to do
before we eat.

THE VENUS.
Put yr hand here.

THE BARON DOCTEUR.
Yr warm.

THE VENUS.
Yes.

THE BARON DOCTEUR.
Upset stomach? I'll fix you something.
You eat too many chockluts you know.
I give em to you by the truckload but
you dont have to eat them all.
Practice some restraint.
Drink this.

THE VENUS.
Put yr hand here, Sweetheart.

THE BARON DOCTEUR.
Drink this first.

THE VENUS.
No. Feel me.

THE BARON DOCTEUR.
Fine.

THE VENUS.
THE BARON DOCTEUR.
THE VENUS.
THE BARON DOCTEUR.

(Rest.)

THE BARON DOCTEUR.
What am I feeling?

THE VENUS.
Guess.

THE VENUS.
THE BARON DOCTEUR.

THE VENUS.
THE BARON DOCTEUR.
(She's pregnant.)
(Rest.)

THE BARON DOCTEUR.
God. Is there anything we can do about it?
Ive a wife. A career.
A reputation. Is there anything
we can do about it we together in
the privacy of my office.
Ive got various equipments in there
we could figure something out.

THE VENUS.
THE VENUS.
THE VENUS.

THE VENUS.
Where I come from
its cause for celebration.

THE BARON DOCTEUR.
A simple yes or no will do, Girl.
(Rest.)

THE VENUS.
Yes.

THE BARON DOCTEUR.
Fine.
We'll take care of it this evening.
After dinner.
Is that all right?

THE VENUS.
Yes thats fine.

THE BARON DOCTEUR.
Fine.

THE VENUS.
THE BARON DOCTEUR.

(Rest.)

(She exits.)

THE BARON DOCTEUR.
THE BARON DOCTEUR.

(Rest.)

(The Grade-School Chum appears as if out of thin air.)

THE GRADE-SCHOOL CHUM.
THE BARON DOCTEUR.
THE GRADE-SCHOOL CHUM.
THE BARON DOCTEUR.

THE GRADE-SCHOOL CHUM.
The door was wide open.
I walked right in.
You 2 should keep yr voices down.
Everyone kin hear yr business.
(Rest.)
Dont you recognize me?

THE BARON DOCTEUR.
Cant say I do.

THE GRADE-SCHOOL CHUM.
We went to school together.
Remember?
(Rest.)

131

THE BARON DOCTEUR.
THE GRADE-SCHOOL CHUM.

(Rest.)

THE BARON DOCTEUR.
Vaguely.

THE GRADE-SCHOOL CHUM.
I was the one who ripped the wings off the flies.
We were like brothers.
Hug me!

THE BARON DOCTEUR.
Beat it.

THE GRADE-SCHOOL CHUM.
Whats that thing around yr neck?

THE BARON DOCTEUR.
None of yr business.

THE GRADE-SCHOOL CHUM.
Get rid of her.
Shes not yr type.

THE BARON DOCTEUR.
Good evening, Sir.
I'll show you out.

THE GRADE-SCHOOL CHUM.
Yr wifes distraught.

THE BARON DOCTEUR.
No she is not!

THE GRADE-SCHOOL CHUM.
Yr reputation is in shambles.

THE BARON DOCTEUR.
My discoveriesll right that.

THE GRADE-SCHOOL CHUM.
You better publish those discoveries soon, Old Friend,
The Academy wont wait for ever.

THE BARON DOCTEUR.
I'll dissect her soon enough!

THE GRADE-SCHOOL CHUM.
Ive come as a friend.
Giving friendly advice.

THE BARON DOCTEUR.
Friend.
To her I am a mere
Anatomical Columbus.
Lemme read you a little
of what Ive written so far.
Where to begin? *Uh hehm.*
(He reads from his notebook.)
(("... the vast protuberance of her buttocks ...
the somewhat brutish appearance of her face."))

THE GRADE-SCHOOL CHUM.
So, get rid of her!
Break with her!
Kick her out on her fat ass!

THE BARON DOCTEUR.
But, I
I love her.
I love her!!

Scene 8
"For the Love of The Venus,"
Act III, Scene 9

The Negro Resurrectionist is the only audience.

The Uncle presents The Bride-To-Be disguised as The Hottentot Venus.

THE UNCLE.
Presenting.
Presenting.
Young Man, to you for love alone
The Wild Thing of yr hearts desire:
From the darkest jungles may I present: "The Hottentot
    Venus!"

THE YOUNG MAN.
THE BRIDE-TO-BE AS THE HOTTENTOT VENUS.
THE YOUNG MAN.
THE BRIDE-TO-BE AS THE HOTTENTOT VENUS.

(Rest.)

THE FATHER.
Young Man, say something.

THE YOUNG MAN.
Good god good God.
She is so odd.
Love?
Youre Love?

THE BRIDE-TO-BE AS THE HOTTENTOT VENUS.
THE YOUNG MAN.

THE BRIDE-TO-BE AS THE HOTTENTOT VENUS.
THE YOUNG MAN.

(Rest.)

THE YOUNG MAN.
She doesnt speak?

THE UNCLE.
Not many words we understand.
Her hometown lingos uh strange one.
Therefore, Hottentot Venus darling,
allow me to interpret.
(Rest.)
Hottentot Venus, you speak first.
(Rest.)
(They click and cluck at each other.)

THE UNCLE.
THE BRIDE-TO-BE AS THE HOTTENTOT VENUS.

(Rest.)

THE UNCLE.
Young Man, she says shes Love.

THE YOUNG MAN.
Whisper, ask her, if shes wild.
(More clicking. More clucking.)

THE UNCLE.
THE HOTTENTOT VENUS.

(Rest.)

THE UNCLE.
She sez she comes from far uhway where its quite hot.
She sez shes pure bred Hottentot.

She sez if wilds your desire
she comes from The Wilds and she carries them behind her.
[Wild is her back ground her fundament so to speek
and although shes grown accoustomed to our civil ways
she still holds the Wilds within her
behind, inside, infront
which is to say, that all yr days
with her will be a lively lovely bliss.]

THE YOUNG MAN.
Let me look at her!

THE UNCLE.
Circle around
get all her angles.

(The Young Man orbits briefly.)

THE YOUNG MAN.
THE BRIDE-TO-BE AS THE HOTTENTOT VENUS.
THE YOUNG MAN.

(He stares hard at her. Tableau.)

THE NEGRO RESURRECTIONIST.
"The height, measured after death,
was 4 feet 11 and 1/2 inches.
The total weight of the body was 98 pounds *avoirdupois* ...
The great amounts of subcutaneous fat were
quite suprising."
(Rest.)
Scene #7:

Scene 7
She'll Make a Splendid Corpse

Bright sunshine.

The Venus in her bedroom daydreaming. She wears a wig.

THE VENUS.
He spends all his time with me because he loves me.
He hardly visits her at all.
She may be his wife all right but shes all dried up.
He is not thuh most thrilling lay Ive had, but his gold makes
    up thuh difference and hhhh
I love him.
He will leave that wife for good and we'll get married (we
    better or I'll make a scene) oh, we'll get married.
And we will lie in bed and make love all day long.
Hahahaha.
We'll set tongues wagging for the rest of the century.
The Doctor will introduce me to Napoléon himself: Oh,
    yes yr Royal Highness the Negro question does keep me
    awake at night oh yes it does.
Servant girl! Do this and that!
When I'm Mistress I'll be a tough cookie.
I'll rule the house with an iron fist and have the most
    wonderful parties.
Society will seek me out: Wheres Venus? Right here!
Hhhhh. I need uh new wig.
Every afternoon I'll take a 3 hour bath. In hot rosewater.
After my bath theyll pat me down.
20 servants will attend me.
Theyll rub my body with the most expensive oils
    perfume my big buttocks and sprinkle them with gold dust!

(The Baron Docteur enters and watches her.)

Come here quick, slave and attend me!
Fetch my sweets! Fix my hair!
Do this do that do this do that!
Hahahahahahah! Mmmmmmm.

THE BARON DOCTEUR.
What are you doing?

THE VENUS.
Oh.
Im sunning myself.

THE BARON DOCTEUR.
Then you should have a parasol.

THE VENUS.
No thanks.
Kiss me.

THE BARON DOCTEUR.
Little Hotsey-Totsey.

THE VENUS.
Come to bed.

THE BARON DOCTEUR.
Its the middle of the day.

THE VENUS.
So?

THE BARON DOCTEUR.
Mmmm.

THE VENUS.
THE BARON DOCTEUR.

THE VENUS.
I dont think I wanna go to yr Academy inny more.

THE BARON DOCTEUR.
Dont be silly.
They all love you there.
And yr French is brilliant.
Its only been 2 years and yr sounding like a native.
Yr a linguistic genius!
Everybody agrees.

THE VENUS.
They touch me sometimes.
When yr not looking.

THE BARON DOCTEUR.
How could they not?
Touching you is — well, its their job.

THE VENUS.
Theyre lascivious.

THE BARON DOCTEUR.
Jesus.
Dont be hyperbolic.

THE VENUS.
You seem half there.
Love me?
(Rest.)

THE BARON DOCTEUR.
THE VENUS.

(Rest.)

THE BARON DOCTEUR.
Im here arent I?

THE VENUS.
I'll wake up one day youll be gone.

THE BARON DOCTEUR.
Wrong.
Im here to stay.
Things are just a little off at work thats all.

THE VENUS.
Touch me
down here.

THE BARON DOCTEUR.
What is it?

THE VENUS.
THE BARON DOCTEUR.

(Rest.)
(Shes pregnant again.)

THE BARON DOCTEUR.
Can we do anything? Oh God.

THE VENUS.
Oh God.

THE BARON DOCTEUR.
A simple yes or no will do.

THE VENUS.
Im not feeling very well.
Its hot in here.
Love me?

THE BARON DOCTEUR.
A simple yes or no will do, Girl!

THE VENUS.
Yes.
Yes.

THE BARON DOCTEUR.
Good. Not get some sleep.

THE VENUS.
THE BARON DOCTEUR.

(Rest.)

THE VENUS.
Whats "maceration."

THE BARON DOCTEUR.
Huh?

THE VENUS.
"Maceration."

THE BARON DOCTEUR.
Whyd you ask?

THE VENUS.
They always say:
"the measurementsll be corrected after
'maceration.'" Whats it mean?

THE BARON DOCTEUR.
"Macerations" French for "lunch."
"After Lunch" we also say.
(Rest.)
Yr my true Love.
Now get some sleep.

(They sleep. Enter The Grade-School Chum. As if in a dream. The Baron Docteur wakes up with a start.)

141

THE GRADE-SCHOOL CHUM.
Ready?
Cough.

THE BARON DOCTEUR.
Uhh!

THE GRADE-SCHOOL CHUM.
Turn yr head.
Cough uhgain.

THE BARON DOCTEUR.
Uhh!
Yr not my regular physician.

THE GRADE-SCHOOL CHUM.
Nope.
Say "Aaaah."

THE BARON DOCTEUR.
"Aaaah."

THE GRADE-SCHOOL CHUM.
Bigger.

THE BARON DOCTEUR.
"Aaaaaaah?"
(Rest.)
Shes my True Love.
She'd make uh splendid wife.

THE GRADE-SCHOOL CHUM.
Yr sick.

THE BARON DOCTEUR.
Thatsright.

THE GRADE-SCHOOL CHUM.
Whatwith?

THE BARON DOCTEUR.
True Love.

THE GRADE-SCHOOL CHUM.
Yr reputation is in shambles.

THE BARON DOCTEUR.
So?

THE GRADE-SCHOOL CHUM.
Yr wifes distraught.

THE BARON DOCTEUR.
Oh, she is not!

THE GRADE-SCHOOL CHUM.
Whats so great about the black girl tell me.

THE BARON DOCTEUR.
Get lost.

THE GRADE-SCHOOL CHUM.
Yr still childless with the Mrs. arent you.

THE BARON DOCTEUR.
Beat it.

THE GRADE-SCHOOL CHUM.
And a laughing stock of the Academy to boot.
Whats that uhround yr neck?

THE BARON DOCTEUR.
Uh charm. For luck. Get lost.

THE GRADE-SCHOOL CHUM.
Here take a pill. Doctors orders.
Itll clear yr head.
Go on. Doctors orders.
Take it now.
Wash it down.
Aaaah?

THE BARON DOCTEUR.
Aaah.

(The Grade-School Chum tosses the pill in The Baron Docteur's mouth and The Baron Docteur swallows it down. The Grade-School Chum studies the amulet.)

THE GRADE-SCHOOL CHUM.
Yr breath is off. Smells like — woah: fuck.
I wouldnt wear that. Looks like bad luck.

THE BARON DOCTEUR.
You think?

THE GRADE-SCHOOL CHUM.
I do. Lets take it off.
Im doing you a favor, Man:
Im packing yr bags and Im bringing you with me.

THE BARON DOCTEUR.
Do I have a choice?

THE GRADE-SCHOOL CHUM.
Sure.
But you know, of course,
yr not the only Doc
Whos got hisself uh Hottentot.

THE BARON DOCTEUR.
THE GRADE-SCHOOL CHUM.

144

THE BARON DOCTEUR.
Speak plainly, Friend.

THE GRADE-SCHOOL CHUM.
Some chap in Germany or somethin
Got his hands on one.
He performed the autopsy today.
Word is he'll publish inny minute.

THE BARON DOCTEUR.
He'll beat me to the punch!

THE GRADE-SCHOOL CHUM.
What do you care
yr in Luv.

THE BARON DOCTEUR.
THE GRADE-SCHOOL CHUM.

THE BARON DOCTEUR.
Shes not feeling so well.
Said so herself.

THE GRADE-SCHOOL CHUM.
She'll probably outlive us all.

THE BARON DOCTEUR.
Shes —
Shes got the clap.

THE GRADE-SCHOOL CHUM.
The clap?
From you?

THE BARON DOCTEUR.
Perhaps.
(Rest.)

It makes my work with her
Indecent somehow.

THE GRADE-SCHOOL CHUM.
"Indecency!"
We could clap her into jail for that.

THE BARON DOCTEUR.
We could?

THE GRADE-SCHOOL CHUM.
Its up to you of course.
(Rest.)
Remember who you are, Sir,
and make the right decision.
Say yes and we'll have her gone by morning.

THE BARON DOCTEUR.
There must be some other solution.

THE GRADE-SCHOOL CHUM.
We'll clap her into jail.
And if her clap runs its course, well,
Thats fate, Friend.

THE BARON DOCTEUR.
Oh God.

THE GRADE-SCHOOL CHUM.
A simple yes or no will do, Doctor.
Come on.

THE BARON DOCTEUR.
Such a lovely creature in her way.
She has a grace —

THE GRADE-SCHOOL CHUM.
Come on.
Say yes.
Before she wakes.

THE BARON DOCTEUR.
Her charming hands —

THE GRADE-SCHOOL CHUM.
Shes just a 2-bit sideshow freak.

THE BARON DOCTEUR.
She would have made uh splendid wife.

THE GRADE-SCHOOL CHUM.
Oh, please.
She'll make uh splendid corpse.

(The Grade-School Chum exits leading The Baron Docteur by the hand. The Venus wakes up with a start. She is alone.)

THE VENUS.
THE VENUS.
THE VENUS.
THE VENUS.

(Rest.)

THE VENUS.
Is it uh little hot in here
Or is it just me?

(Rest.)

THE VENUS.
THE VENUS.
THE VENUS.
THE VENUS.

(A knot of Spectators gather around her.)

THE CHORUS OF SPECTATORS.
Lookie-Lookie-Lookie-Lookie
Hubba-Hubba-Hubba-Hubba
Lookie-Lookie-Lookie-Lookie
Hubba-Hubba-Hubba-Hubba

THE CHORUS OF THE SPECTATORS.
THE VENUS.
THE CHORUS OF THE SPECTATORS.

(The Chorus of the Spectators bursts into a riot. The Venus flees.)

THE NEGRO RESURRECTIONIST.
Order!
Order!
Order!
Order!

(Suddenly The Venus is again imprisoned chained like a dog in the yard. The Negro Resurrectionist seats himself beside her. He is her guard.)

THE VENUS.
THE NEGRO RESURRECTIONIST.
THE VENUS.
THE NEGRO RESURRECTIONIST.

THE GRADE-SCHOOL CHUM.
Indecency!
So clap her into jail for that!

THE BARON DOCTEUR.
Clap her into jail for that?

(The Chorus of the Spectators applaud.)

148

Scene 6
Some Years Later, at Tübingen (Reprise)

The Chorus of the Spectators applaud.

The Baron Docteur reads from his notebook.

THE BARON DOCTEUR.
Uh hehm:
(Rest.)
"In regards to the formation of her buttocks
we make the following remarks:
The fatty cushion, a.k.a.
Steatopygia was 9 inches deep. Her buttocks —"

THE NEGRO RESURRECTIONIST.
Scene #6:
Several years later at a Conference in Tübingen
The Dis(-re-)memberment of The Venus Hottentot Part II:

THE BARON DOCTEUR.
"Her buttocks had nearly
nearly the usual origin and insertion
but the muscular fibres were suprisingly thin and flabby
and very badly developed thus showing that
the protuberance of the buttocks
so peculiar to the Bushman race
is not the result of any muscular development but rather
totally dependent
on the accumulation of fat."
(Rest.)

(The Venus is chained. The Negro Ressurectionist stands watch.)

THE VENUS.
You ever Love?

THE NEGRO RESURRECTIONIST.
Naw.

THE VENUS.
No?

THE NEGRO RESURRECTIONIST.
Nope.

THE VENUS.
Ever been loved?

THE NEGRO RESURRECTIONIST.
Uh uhnnn.
(He gives her a red heart box of chocolates.)
(Rest.)
Chockluts. Here.
Theyre not from me.
Theyre from a man who sez he knew you when.
Doctor I think he sed.

THE VENUS.
"Doctor?"

THE NEGRO RESURRECTIONIST.
Maybe once when you were sick?

(Rest.)

(The Baron Docteur continues with great difficulty.)

THE BARON DOCTEUR.
Oh God my mind was wandering
Where was I?
Uh hehm:

"While the uterus had the ordinary form of that organ in a
once or twice impregnated female,
The external characters,
especially of the reproductive organs,
form, in this view, the centerpiece of Study.
(Rest.)
The *labia majora* were small.
The clitoris sized moderate to large
and had a well-developed *prepuce*
all situated far more conspicuously
than in the European female.
(Rest.)
Her most remarkable features were the long appendages
which hung down from her *pudendum.*
They resembled 2 thongs
each about the thickness of a cedar-wood pencil.
Exactly like strips of sheepskin, slightly twisted,
and aparently vascular. On separating her *labia*
I found the *appendages to be the nymphae elongated.*
I took up her appendages
And led the right one round her right side
Above her gluteal projection,
Similary
I led her left appendage round her left side
And their ends met at her spine.
(Rest.)
There was no trace of hymen.
(Rest.)
(Rest.)
The remarkable development of the *labia minora*
which heretofore is so general a characteristic of
the Hottentot or Bushman race
was so sufficiently well marked that it well distinguished itself
from those of any of the ordinary varieties of the human
    species.
Again, their difference was so marked
their formation so distinguished
that they formed this studys centerpiece.

This author recommends further examination of said
    formation."
(Rest.)
Thank you.

(He stands there holding his notebook and hanging his head.)

Scene 5
Who Is She To Me?

The Venus sleeps. The Negro Resurrectionist stands watch.

THE GRADE-SCHOOL CHUM.
You watch The Venus Hottentot?

THE NEGRO RESURRECTIONIST.
Im her Watchman, thats right.
And I'll put her safely in the ground when she dies too.
Whats that to you?

THE GRADE-SCHOOL CHUM.
I recognize you, Man
I know you from way back.
Youve got a memorable face.

THE NEGRO RESURRECTIONIST.
So what.

THE GRADE-SCHOOL CHUM.
You used to unearth bodies
for my postmortem class.
An illegal craft as I remember.

THE NEGRO RESURRECTIONIST.
I quit that line years ago.

THE GRADE-SCHOOL CHUM.
Once a *digger* always one.

THE NEGRO RESURRECTIONIST.
Get to the point.

THE GRADE-SCHOOL CHUM.
A friend of mine in the medical profession
is very interested in the body of yr ward.
After she "goes on"
For scientific analysis only of course.

THE NEGRO RESURRECTIONIST.
No thank you.

THE GRADE-SCHOOL CHUM.
I'll have to call the cops on you.
Theyll lock you up.

THE NEGRO RESURRECTIONIST.
I quit that buisiness!

THE GRADE-SCHOOL CHUM.
Yd be surprised at how
the legal system works.
(Rest.)
Shes gonna kick it inny minute.
We'll pay you for yr trouble.
Its not for me but for a friend.
He doesnt got the balls to ask.

(The Grade-School Chum knees him in the balls.)

We'll pay you well. In gold.
Say yes.

THE NEGRO RESURRECTIONIST.
THE GRADE-SCHOOL CHUM.

(Rest.)

THE NEGRO RESURRECTIONIST.
Uh uhnn.

THE GRADE-SCHOOL CHUM.
Then its thuh slammer, Stupid.
I gotcha by thuh throat, admit it.

THE NEGRO RESURRECTIONIST.
THE GRADE-SCHOOL CHUM.
THE NEGRO RESURRECTIONIST.
THE GRADE-SCHOOL CHUM.

(Rest.)

THE NEGRO RESURRECTIONIST.
Ok.
I mean, whatever.
Yr uh bastards bastard.
But fine. All right, I guess.
I mean, who is she to me?

THE GRADE-SCHOOL CHUM.
THE NEGRO RESURRECTIONIST.

THE GRADE-SCHOOL CHUM.
Theres a good boy. Heh-Heh-Heh.
Heres a little in advance.

(The Grade-School Chum tosses The Negro Resurrectionist a single gold coin. He takes the coin but feels like shit.)

Theres a good boy. Heh-Heh-Heh.
Heres a little in advance.

Scene 4
"For the Love of The Venus" (Conclusion)

The Baron Docteur watches from one place, The Venus from another. The Bride-To-Be masquerades as The Hottentot Venus and The Young Man stares at her.

THE BRIDE-TO-BE AS THE HOTTENTOT VENUS.
THE YOUNG MAN.
THE BRIDE-TO-BE AS THE HOTTENTOT VENUS.
THE YOUNG MAN.
(Rest.)

THE YOUNG MAN.
Tell her I'm smitten.

THE UNCLE.
I think she knows.

THE YOUNG MAN.
By these knees Im bending on
True Venus Im forever thine.
I'll never change.
Promise me the same.
Uncle, put that on yr tongue then in her tongue then in
    her ear.
(Rest.)
What is her answer?

THE UNCLE.
She promises constancy but
as we loose uh skin layer every day
so will she shrug her old self off.

THE YOUNG MAN.
Shrug all you want but keep thuh core.

(Rest.)
Answer.

(Rest.)

(Astounding metamorphosis! She removes her disguise.)

THE BRIDE-TO-BE.
Dearheart: your true love stands before you.

(The Young Man gives The Bride-To-Be a red heart box of chocolates. Love tableau. Curtain. The Baron Docteur applauds.)

Scene 3
A Brief History of Chocolate

THE VENUS.
(Rest.)
A BRIEF HISTORY OF CHOCOLATE:
It is written in the ancient chronicles that the Gods one day
    looked down with pity.
Pity on the people as they struggled.
The Gods resolved to visit the people
and teach them the ways of Love
for Love helps in times of hardship.
As an act of Love one God gives to the people
a little shrub that had, until then, belongd
only to the Gods.
This was the cacao tree.
(Rest.)
Time passed.
Time passed uhgain:
We find ourselves in the 19th Century.
The Aztec word *cacao* literally "food of the Gods"
becomes *chocolate* and *cocoa.*

The *cacao* bean, once used as money
becomes an exotic beverage.
Chocolate was soon mixed with milk and sugar
and formed into lozenges which one could eat on the run.
Chocolate lozenges are now found in a variety of shapes
mixed with everything from nuts to brandy.
Chocolate is a recognized emotional stimulant,
for doctors have recently noticed the tendency of some
persons,
especially women,
to go on chocolate binges
binges either *after* emotionally upsetting incidents
or in an effort to allow themselves *to handle* an incident
which may be emotionally upsetting.
This information is interesting in that it has become the
practice
to present a gift of chocolates when professing Love.
This practice, begun some time ago, continues to this day.
(Rest.)
While chocolate was once used as a stimulant and source of
nutrition
it is primarily today a great source of fat,
And, of course, pleasure.

Scene 2
The Venus Hottentot Tells the Story of Her Life

The Negro Resurrectionist fingers his new gold coin.

THE VENUS.
Whered ya get that?

THE NEGRO RESURRECTIONIST.
I found it.
Just this morning on the street.

THE VENUS.
Yr lucky.

THE NEGRO RESURRECTIONIST.
Im not lying!!

THE VENUS.
I didnt say you were.

THE VENUS.
THE NEGRO RESURRECTIONIST.
THE VENUS.
THE NEGRO RESURRECTIONIST.

(Rest.)

THE VENUS.
How long you lived here?

THE NEGRO RESURRECTIONIST.
Me? Ive lived in this town all my life.
I used to dig up people
dead ones. You know,
after theyd been buried.
Doctors pay a lot for corpses
but "Resurrection" is illegal
And I was always this close to getting arrested.
This Jail-Watchman jobs much more carefree.

THE VENUS.
You dont have anything you miss?
Yr lucky, Watchman.
I always dream of home
in every spare minute.
It was a shitty shitty life but oh I miss it.
Whats that sound outside, crowds?

THE NEGRO RESURRECTIONIST.
Yes.
Yr still a star.

THE VENUS.
Dont let them in.

THE NEGRO RESURRECTIONIST.
Dont worry.

THE VENUS.
THE NEGRO RESURRECTIONIST.
THE VENUS.
THE NEGRO RESURRECTIONIST.

(Rest.)

THE VENUS.
Whats that outside?
Crowds?

THE NEGRO RESURRECTIONIST.
Just rain.
We're having lousy weather.
Its just rain.

THE VENUS.
I was born near the coast, Watchman.
Journeyed some worked some
ended up here.
I would live here I thought but only for uh minute!
Make a mint.
Had plans to.
He had a beard.
Big bags of money!
Where wuz I?
Fell in love. Hhh.
Tried my hand at French.

Gave me a haircut
and thuh claps
you get thuh picture, huh?
Dont look at me
dont look ...
(Rest.)
(She dies.)

THE NEGRO RESURRECTIONIST.
(Rest.)
"Early in the 19th century a poor wretched woman was
exhibited in England under the appelation of *The Hottentot
Venus.* With an intensely ugly figure, distorted beyond all
European notions of beauty, she was said to possess precisely
the kind of shape which is most admired among her country-
men, the Hottentots."

The year was 1810, three years after the Bill for the Abolition
of the Slave-Trade had been pased in Parliament, and among
protests and denials, horror and fascination Her show went
on. She died in Paris 5 years later: a plaster cast of her body
was once displayed, along with her skeleton, at the *Musee de
l'Homme.*

(Rest.)

Scene 1
Final Chorus

THE NEGRO RESURRECTIONIST.
I regret to inform you that Thuh Venus Hottentot iz dead.

ALL.
Dead!

THE NEGRO RESURRECTIONIST.
There wont be inny show tuhnite.

THE VENUS.
Miss me Miss me Miss me.

THE GRADE-SCHOOL CHUM.
Exposure iz what killed her
nothin on in our cold weather.

THE NEGRO RESURRECTIONIST.
23 days in uh row it rained.

THE BARON DOCTEUR.
I say she died of drink.

THE NEGRO RESURRECTIONIST.
It was the cold I think.

THE VENUS.
Hear ye hear ye hear ye
Thuh Venus Hottentot iz dead.
There wont be inny show tuhnite.

THE GRADE-SCHOOL CHUM.
I know yr dissuhpointed.
I hate tuh let you down.

ALL.
Gimmie gimmie back my buck!

THE VENUS.
I come from miles and miles and miles and miles

ALL.
Hotsey-Totsey!

THE NEGRO RESURRECTIONIST.
Diggidy-diggidy-diggidy-diggidy

ALL.
Diggidy-diggidy-diggidy-dawg.

THE CHORUS.
Turn uhway
dont look
Cover yr face
Cover yr eyes.

ALL.
Drum Drum Drum Drum
Hur-ry Hur-ry Step in Step in
(Rest.)
Thuh Venus Hottentot iz dead.

THE VENUS.
Tail end of the tale for there must be uh end.
Is that Venus, Black Goddess was shameless, she sinned, or
    else
Completely unknowing thuh Godfearin ways, she stood
Showing her ass off in her iron cage.
When Death met Love Death deathd Love
and left Love tuh rot
Au naturel end for Thuh Miss Hottentot.
Loves soul, which was tidy, hides in heaven, yes, thats it
Loves corpse stands on show in museum. Please visit.

ALL.
Diggidy-diggidy-diggidy
Diggidy-diggidy-diggidy-dawg!

THE NEGRO RESURRECTIONIST.
A Scene of Love:

THE VENUS.
Kiss me *Kiss* me *Kiss* me *Kiss*

162

GLOSSARY OF MEDICAL TERMS

ANNULAR LIGAMENT — a large muscle in the wrist

ATLAS — the part of the spine that supports the head

ATTOLENS and ATTRAHENS AUREM — the muscles of the ear

AVOIRDUPOIS — personal weight

AXILLA — the armpit

CALVARIUM — the skull lacking the lower jaw

CERVICALIS ASCENDENS — a neck muscle near the upper ribs

CLAVICLE — the collar bone

COCCYX — the tail bone

CONJUNCTIVA — mucous membrane lining the eyeball

DORSO-EPITROCHLEAR MUSCLE — a muscle similar to the LATISSIMUS DORSI found in nonhuman animals

DORSUM — the back surface of an area

EXTENSOR COMMUNIS DIGITORUM — a muscle of the forearm

EXTENSOR MINIMI DIGITI — a slender muscle running through the arm and into the hand

EXTENSOR PRIMI INTERNODIL POLLICIS — the smallest muscle of the arm

FASCIA — a sheet of connective tissue

FEMUR — the thigh bone (the longest, largest and strongest bone in the skeleton)

FLEXOR BREVIS DIGITORUM PEDIS — a muscle in the middle of the sole of the foot

FORMAL CARTILAGE'S TIP — a.k.a. the xyphoid process, the cartilage at the tip of the breastbone

FUNDUS — part of the aperture of an organ

GLUTEUS MAXIMUS — the muscle of the buttocks

GLUTEUS MEDIUS — the muscle on the outer surface of the pelvis covered by GLUTEUS MAXIMUS

HUMERAL BONE — the upper arm bone

LABIA MAJORA — the outer vaginal lips

LABIA MINORA — the inner vaginal lips

LATISSIMUS DORSI MUSCLE — a large flat muscle covering the lumbar and lower half of the dorsal region

LEVATOR ANGULI SCAPULAE — a muscle at the back and side of the neck

LEVATOR CLAVICULAE — a muscle of the clavicle area first noted by Dr. McWhinnie

MALAR — two small bones forming the prominence of the cheek

MAMMAE — the breasts

MASTOID PROCESS — the bone behind the ear, part of the jaw

METACARPO-PHALANGEAL — the hand and finger bones

NYMPHAE — the inner lips of the vulva

OCCIPITALIS MUSCLE — the muscle at the back of the skull

OMO-HYOID — a muscle of the neck, passing across the side of the neck

OS CAICIS — the heel bone

PATELLA — the knee bone

PELVIS AT CREST OF ILIUM — the top crest of the hip bone

PERINEUM — the muscle between genitals and anus

PREPUCE — the folds of skin enveloping the clitoris

PUBES — the pubic region

PUDENDUM — external genital organs, especially of a woman

RADIUS — the arm bone on the thumb side

SACRO-LUMBALIS MUSCLE — located in the external portion of the erector (lower) spine

SCAPULA — the bone comprising the back part of the shoulder

SEPTUM — the inner wall of the nose separating the nostrils

SEPTUM NARIUM/NARES — the inner nasal area

SERRATUS MAGNUS — a muscle in the chest

SPLENIUS COLLI — a muscle at the back of the neck

STEATOPYGIA — an excessive development of fat on the buttocks especially of females, which is common among the so-called Hottentots and some Negro peoples

STERNO-MASTOID — a large muscle passing downwards along the front of the neck

STERNUM — the breastbone

TERES MINOR — the narrow muscle of the shoulder area

THORAX — the chest cavity

TIBIA — the leg bone between the knee and ankle

TRACHELO-MASTOID — a muscle running from the jaw area around to the back

TRAGUS — the prominence at the front of the opening of the ear

TRANSVERSE PROCESS — a muscular-like lever which serves as the attachment of muscles which move the different parts of the spine

TRAPEZIUS — a muscle covering the upper and back part of the neck and shoulders

TRICEPS — muscles situated on the back of the arm

TROCHANTERS — the upper part of the thigh bone

TUBERCLE — the protuberance near the head of the rib

ULNA — the arm bone on the little finger side

UMBILICUS — the belly button

VERTEX — the top of the head

GLOSSARY OF CHOCOLATES

BOUCHON FRAISE — cupcake-shaped, either dark chocolate or buttercream, filled with either strawberry crème fraîche or cognac flavor, respectively

CAPEZZOLI DI VENERE — "the nipples of Venus," breast-shaped mounds in dark or light chocolate with a red or white iced "nipple" on top; crème fraîche often inside

ENFANT DE BRUXELLES — dark chocolate lozenge with an image of a little African child stamped upon it; coffee and chocolate crème fraîche inside

ESCARGOT LAIT — fashioned in the shape of a snail's shell; milk chocolate with praliné inside

PETITS COEURS — "little hearts" of solid chocolate

PHARAON — a solid lozenge, either dark or buttercream, with the image of a pharaoh's head stamped upon it

RHUM CARAMEL — cube-shaped, dark chocolate with light caramel; crème fraîche and rum flavor inside

PROPERTY LIST

Scrub brush (THE GIRL)
Bucket (THE GIRL)
Bucket (THE MOTHER-SHOWMAN)
Brush (THE MOTHER-SHOWMAN)
Banner: THE VENUS HOTTENTOT
Stick (THE MOTHER-SHOWMAN)
Feather amulet (THE VENUS, THE BARON DOCTEUR)
Letters (THE GRADE-SCHOOL CHUM)
Hottentot Venus doll (THE NEGRO RESURRECTIONIST)
Scissors (THE BARON DOCTEUR)
Pill (THE GRADE-SCHOOL CHUM)
3-legged stool (THE NEGRO RESURRECTIONIST)
Gold coin (THE GRADE-SCHOOL CHUM, THE NEGRO
        RESURRECTIONIST)